The Protection
of our English Churches

FIG 1 *North Cerney, Glos, photographed by Will Croome in August 1949; the ideal at which the CCCC aimed (compare Fig 19). (Photograph in CCC collection.)*

The Protection of our English Churches

The History of the Council for the
Care of Churches 1921–1996

Donald Findlay

COUNCIL FOR THE CARE OF CHURCHES

ISBN 0 7151 7575 0

Published 1996 by the Council for the Care of Churches

© *The Central Board of Finance of the Church of England 1996*

Acknowledgements
Extracts from The Book of Common Prayer, the rights in which are vested in the Crown, are reproduced by permission of the Crown's Patentee, Cambridge University Press.

Extracts from C. Lycett Green (ed.) *John Betjeman: Letters, Vol. I, 1926–51* (Methuen, 1994): *Vol II, 1951–84* (Methuen, 1995) are reprinted by permission of Reed Consumer Books.

Printed in England by The Longdunn Press Ltd, Bristol

Cover Photograph: *The Church of St George, Dunster, Somerset, the town where the Council was based 1939–55. Photograph by Derek Forss, Landscape Photography.*

To Judith
with gratitude

When a teacher of the law has become a learner in the kingdom
of Heaven, he is like a householder who can produce from his
store things new and old.

Matthew 13. 52
(Revised English Bible)

Contents

List of illustrations

Preface

When the west door was thrown open, Mr Davidson could not repress an exclamation of pleased surprise at the completeness and richness of the interior. Screenwork, pulpit, seating and glass – all were of the same period; and as he advanced into the nave and sighted the organ-case with its gold-embossed pipes in the western gallery, his cup of satisfaction was filled.[1]

Thus, in his ghost story *The Uncommon Prayer Book*, the distinguished medievalist and bibliographer M.R. James imagines an antiquarian, given an unexpected free week at the beginning of January, setting off to visit the churches of the Tent valley on 'a pearl of a day too fine to be spent indoors', and arriving at the church beside the uninhabited Brockstone Court. It is a seventeenth-century building, effectively the chapel of the house, and the story hinges on the fact that every time the gamekeeper's wife, who acts as caretaker, goes into the building she finds the prayerbooks in the family pew, which she left neatly closed on her previous visit, lying open to display a curious rubric.

Clearly Davidson is no narrow medievalist, for the church which calls forth his spontaneous admiration is Laudian. Nor is his interest in churches only art historical, for he inquires about its present use. James might have been describing F.C. Eeles, the first Secretary of the Council for the Care of Churches, on one of his thousands of church visits, or an early member of a Diocesan Advisory Committee deputed to report on a distant church in the diocese hitherto unknown to him. For Eeles was a man with a passionate enthusiasm for preserving the best from the past and introducing the best from the present in order to render churches fit to serve the highest purpose – the worship of Almighty God.

His single-minded yet, at the same time, broad-minded approach has informed the work of the Council during its 75 years of existence. This book is intended to set in context the development of the Council and its work, in relation both to central organisations within and beyond the Church of England, and to the Diocesan Advisory Committees for the Care of Churches (DACs) all over the country. The title is that used for the first seven reports published by the Council.

The presence of an enlightened antiquary such as Mr Davidson in a James ghost story is perhaps no accident, for many of those most closely associated with the Council prove to have hailed from Cambridge, and, indeed from James's own college of King's. The first, third and fourth Chairmen were all King's men, as was Dean Milner-White (Vice-Chairman) and a later Secretary, Peter Burman, while the second Secretary, Ian Rawlins, was at Trinity, the fourth, Desmond Mandeville, at Corpus, and the sixth and present Secretary, Thomas Cocke, at Pembroke. Moreover, the present Chairman of the Cathedrals Fabric Commission for England, Michael McCrum, has recently retired as Master of Corpus, and the Secretary of the CFCE, Richard Gem, was at Peterhouse. Although there were at least two notable Oxonians, Dean Foxley Norris, the second Chairman, of Trinity, and Will Croome, Vice-Chairman, of New College, and more recent Chairmen have been fairly equally divided between the two places, this bias towards Cambridge suggests that the broad distinction established in the 1830s between theology at Oxford and ecclesiology at Cambridge has held to the end of the twentieth century.

In the compilation of this history I have been greatly helped by a number of people, not least by the Council itself which allowed me the time in which to write it. I must first thank Judith Scott for allowing me to see a number of private papers and for useful information about the Council's founding secretary and the greater part of its history; Brenda Hough and her colleagues at the Church of England Record Centre for unfailingly coming up with the answers to my questions; Thomas Cocke and Jonathan Goodchild for reading and commenting on the text, Patricia Davies for seeking out some of the photographs, especially that on the cover, and for guiding me through the finer points of computer technology; all my colleagues both at Fielden House, especially Andrew Argyrakis, Joan Denne, Janet Seeley and Steven Sleight, and at Church House Publishing; and Michael Gillingham, who has been involved with the Council's work for over 30 years, for much help and encouragement.

It was perhaps presumptuous for a Scotsman to take on the task of writing about such an eminently English organisation, but I plead in mitigation that I have worked for the Council for 23 years. Nevertheless such a history ought to be as impartial as possible, and I have tried to write it as an outsider. The surviving evidence is enormous. The Council, in spite of five moves, seems to have discarded nothing. It has preserved all its minute books, together with those of all its committees, sub-committees, working parties, conferences and so forth, a large number of files on general subjects, on technical matters, on artists and craftsmen, on 'objects' as diverse as flags and pewter octagonal-rimmed font bowls, as well as personal correspondence, files on 43 cathedrals, and, above all, the 16,000 or so files on individual parish churches which make up the national survey of churches. Often the minutiae are as fascinating as the broad sweeps. While attempting to offer an overview of the Council's history, concentrating particularly on the early years which are beginning to fade into obscurity, I have used these rich resources to give something of the flavour of the subjects considered and the personalities encountered. I hope that those who feel that more attention should have been paid to some particular topic or person will be forgiving.

Donald Findlay
Fielden House
March 1996

Part 1
The establishment of the advisory system

The first 35 years

1
Background

On 4 November 1921 30 gentlemen met in the Jerusalem Chamber at Westminster Abbey. Clergy and lay, they had been summoned as representatives of the newly formed Diocesan Advisory Committees for the Care of Churches, 19 of which were represented, and as a result of their discussions the first meeting of a Central Committee for the Protection of English Churches and their Treasures, established to co-ordinate the work, was held on 8 December 1922; the Chairman, proposed by Athelstan Riley, was the Rt Revd E.H. Ryle, Dean of Westminster (formerly Bishop of Exeter and Winchester), the Treasurer Sir Cecil Harcourt Smith (Director of the Victoria and Albert Museum) and the Secretary Mr F.C. Eeles (a member of staff at the V&A). This book explains the reasons for the establishment of the CCPECT (later the Central Council for the Care of Churches), describes how the advisory system for the care of churches was established, and traces its subsequent development.

There had been anxiety for some time about the care of English churches.[1] William Morris' founding of the Society for the Protection of Ancient Buildings (SPAB) in 1877 had been stimulated in great part by the over-thorough restoration of churches. Much of the odium was attached to the name of Sir Gilbert Scott, simply because his name was the best known and his work was probably the most extensive of any architect of his generation. But this was not altogether fair because, while he sometimes replaced 'decadent' features such as Perpendicular windows and doorways with more 'correct' Middle Pointed features based on fairly slender evidence, his theoretical writings are generally remarkably preservationist in tone. The stimulus for thorough restoration and rebuilding had been the forceful demands made in the 1830s by A.W.N. Pugin and the Cambridge Camden (later Ecclesiological) Society that liturgical arrangements, particularly in chancels, should follow medieval precedent. Many people had been shocked at the results, such as J.M.Neale's thoroughgoing transformation of St Nicholas, Old Shoreham, in 1839–40 and Salvin's reworking of the Round Church at Cambridge in the following year, both under the guidance of the Society and both intended to conform to its doctrinaire attitude that 'to restore is to recover the original appearance ...

we must, either from existing evidences or from supposition, recover the original scheme of the edifice as conceived by the first builder',[2] which encouraged such major changes as the removal of clearstories and their replacement with steeply pitched 'authentic' roofs of Middle Pointed character.[3]

The work of the great Victorian restorers is well known – Pearson's re-creation of the Romanesque vaults at Stow, Lincolnshire; Burges' new east end for Waltham Abbey, Essex; and Scott's restorations at so many cathedrals. His transformation of Stafford parish church in 1841–2 has often been discussed, and it was his proposals for Tewkesbury Abbey which finally provoked Morris into forming the SPAB. But although he made a name for himself, Morris was a late runner in the field. During the first half of the century church restoration had moved away from being the province of local builders instructed by churchwardens or landowners into the hands of a new professional class of architects. Over a decade before the SPAB came into being, the Royal Institute of British Architects (founded in 1834) had, at the request of some of the most prominent church restorers amongst its members, established in 1864 a Committee on the Conservation of Ancient Architectural Monuments and Remains, intended to oppose harsh or ill-judged restorations. Later that year the Committee published a pamphlet, *General Advice to the Promoters of the Restoration of Ancient Buildings*, which argued for moderation and a respect for original features and weathering, and condemned large-scale reconstructions and removal of features to meet liturgical demands. A parliamentary *Survey of Church Building and Church Restoration*, promoted by A.J. Beresford Hope amongst others, showed that between 1840 and 1875 a large proportion, more than 7,000 (about 80 per cent), of our ancient parish churches had been restored, rebuilt or enlarged.

Independent scrutiny of plans had also been encouraged by the Incorporated Church Building Society (ICBS), established in 1818 to offer grants towards the increase of seating accommodation in parish churches (and therefore encouraging church enlargement). From the start, the ICBS had insisted on the employment of architects, and as time went on it demanded an increasingly preservationist attitude. The growing professionalism of architects also led to greater importance being attached to the role of Diocesan Architects and Surveyors, appointed by the bishops to approve plans. This naturally led to the widespread employment of the Diocesan Architect within his own area; hence, for example, the number of churches restored or rebuilt by Street in Oxfordshire, by C. Hodgson Fowler in County Durham, or by James Fowler in Lincolnshire. Their approach to church restoration naturally varied, but the ICBS was certainly helped in its moderating influence by the growing number of local architectural societies.

Morris' theories owed much of their inspiration to John Ruskin, who had approved of neither the method nor the purpose of restoration advocated by the Ecclesiological Society and who in 1877 had on principle refused the Gold Medal of the Royal Institute of British Architects from the hand of Sir Gilbert Scott, President in that year. The SPAB approach is well exemplified in the church at Inglesham, Wiltshire, where the only visible evidence of the thorough restoration of the fabric by J.T. Micklethwaite over the decade after 1888 is dates carved on some of the replaced beams.

Set alongside the Ruskinian insistence that the effects of the passage of history, visible in the varied texture of an old building, should be respected, the increasingly preservationist approach in the later years of the century is also shown in the attitude towards what were then called 'Renaissance' buildings (which meant those of the sixteenth and seventeenth centuries).

FIG 2 *Inglesham, Wilts, photographed by Will Croome in 1929, showing medieval stonework and screens together with Jacobean and later woodwork retained and restored in the 1880s. (Photograph in CCC collection.)*

Norman Shaw's treatment of St John Leeds, where he retained and adapted the elaborate Jacobean screens, was remarkably sympathetic to a building furnished in a most un-Ecclesiological way. Although many Georgian buildings had been demolished by the middle of the century, some more sensitive architects soon began to appreciate them. When in 1874 it was proposed that the mid-eighteenth-century church of St John at Hampstead should be replaced by a new building, George Gilbert Scott Junior and G.F. Bodley organised a petition, signed by Butterfield, Seddon and Waterhouse amongst others, which stated that 'the proposal to destroy or transform [Hampstead's] principal ornament will be condemned by every man of taste'[4]. In the north J.T. Micklethwaite, reporting in 1879 on the late-eighteenth-century church of St John Wakefield, argued that 'in answer to those who would pull down the old church and build a new one, a very good church could be made of what already existed',[5] and in due course a sympathetic classical chancel was added. G.G. Scott Junior's careful extension of Pembroke College Chapel, Cambridge (1880), is a model of good practice, as is Temple Moore's refurnishing of Kirkandrews-on-Esk, Cumbria (1893).

THE 'ECCLESIASTICAL EXEMPTION'

While informed opinion was developing a more protective attitude towards ancient and post-Reformation churches, and non-ecclesiastical field monuments had been safeguarded by the Ancient Monuments Protection Act 1882, revised in 1900, anxiety was growing that, although the Act excluded from its protection all church buildings in ecclesiastical use, the Church of England still had no system specifically formulated to control the care of its buildings and their contents. Such controls as existed were enshrined in the faculty jurisdiction, an ancient legislative system extending back at least to the early thirteenth century with the twin objects of protecting the parishioners' rights in their parish church and the control of the 'ordinary', usually the bishop, over changes to the fabric, exercised through the chancellor and the archdeacon. But, although chancellors, the judges of the consistory courts, had indeed decided on matters affecting church fabrics and contents such as the allocation of pews or the erection of galleries, altarpieces and organs in the eighteenth century,[6] and the liturgical ornaments demanded by the ritualists in the nineteenth century, their interest was generally limited to such aspects as financial consequences and the effect of such proposals on parishioners' rights. Neither they nor the *ad hoc* commissions which advised them on specific cases, sometimes cited as the forerunners of DACs, had taken any special interest in the artistic or historic aspects of the proposals.

In 1892 the Dean of the Arches, Lord Penzance, had aligned himself with Morris' observation that 'we are only trustees for those who come after us' when he wrote, in a paragraph still quoted by chancellors, that:

> the sacred edifice has a future as well as a past. It belongs not to any one generation, nor are its interests and condition the exclusive care of those who inhabit the parish at any one period of time. It is in entire conformity with this aspect of the parish church that the law has forbidden any structural alterations to be made in it, save those which are approved by a disinterested authority in the person of the Ordinary, whose deputed discretion and judgement we are here to exercise today.[7]

For the first 40 years of its existence the SPAB could only do its best to publicise bad cases of disrespectful treatment of ancient churches, which it did with vigour – churches formed the greater part of its growing casework. The principal complaint was not that churches were being abandoned or neglected, but rather that too many were still suffering from over-enthusiastic restoration of the type advocated years before by the Ecclesiological Society and long since eschewed by 'every man of taste'. As the Central Committee for the Protection of English Churches and their Treasures was later to say in its first Report, 'continual cases of destruction [by over-restoration] and neglect and the low artistic standard of recent work showed that something was lacking'.[8]

The eventual result was that in 1912 a select committee of Parliament recommended that cathedrals, the most conspicuous ecclesiastical treasures, should be taken out of the control of deans and chapters and transferred to state control as monuments of national importance. The resulting Ancient Monuments Bill at first proposed that churches as well as cathedrals should be included within the ancient monuments legislation (as this concerned buildings erected before 1715, only the Church of England was involved). But, after hearing the Church of England's case, and motivated also by fear that the Liberal government might be outvoted on the Bill by the Conservative opposition if churches were included, the First Commissioner of Works, Lord Beauchamp, successfully moved an amendment at the Bill's second reading in the House of Lords which excluded 'an ecclesiastical building which is for the time being used for ecclesiastical purposes' from the definition of 'monument' and thus from the provisions of the Bill as a whole. The Archbishop of Canterbury, Randall Davidson, opened the Bill's third reading on 8 July 1913 by admitting that, 'though speaking generally the control exercised by the ecclesiastical authorities has been well exercised, I do not for a moment claim infallibility for them throughout the years that have gone'.[9] He went on to announce that he and the Archbishop of York had therefore asked the Dean of the Arches, Sir Lewis Dibdin, to

> make inquiry throughout the dioceses of England as to what are the precautions taken by our ecclesiastical courts and judges to secure that no harm shall arise to the ecclesiastical buildings whose value is so immeasurable ... and whether or not it is desirable that we should formulate for our courts any further direction with a view to additional protection or whether that protection is adequately given at present.[10]

Meanwhile the Bill, excluding churches, was enacted as the Ancient Monuments Consolidation and Amendment Act 1913.

The Ancient Monuments (Churches) Committee established by the Archbishops had only three members – Dibdin (1852–1938), who had been chancellor of three dioceses before becoming Dean of the Arches and Auditor of the Chancery Court of York in 1903, and two diocesan chancellors, Sir Alfred Kempe and Sir Charles Chadwyck-Healey, with ten dioceses between them. Their terms of reference were

> to ascertain what steps are taken on the issue of faculties ... to secure due protection, both on archaeological and artistic grounds, for church fabrics which have to undergo repair or in which changes are being made, and to report ... the information acquired, together with any changes which the facts collected might suggest.[11]

Amongst the evidence taken from all the bishops, the other chancellors and a number of architects and antiquaries, a strongly worded paper was quickly presented to the Archbishops by the SPAB on 16 July 1913; it included a list of forty churches where 'destructive work' was alleged to have been 'carried out under a faculty since 1896'.[12]

The report of the Dibdin Committee set out the existing arrangements for the care of churches, explaining that the church building was vested in the incumbent and its contents in the churchwardens, and that the bishop exercised his authority through his chancellor who granted or refused faculties for alterations to it or its furnishings. A major defect emerged. It was found that, where matters of archaeology or aesthetics were concerned, chancellors felt inhibited from exercising their judgement lest they be open to the charge of applying their personal whim. Two-thirds of the chancellors affirmed that, in the case of major works, they ensured that 'an architect of recognised position' recommended the work and supervised it. Further, 'in many dioceses the bishop himself sees the plans' and 'where the bishop possesses archaeological knowledge his criticism of the plans is of great value',[13] and in some places there were diocesan or local societies which could be consulted. But the fact remained that there was no 'uniform or officially recognised machinery by the use of which the court can obtain skilled and independent advice upon archaeological, architectural and artistic questions'.

The Commission established that in half of the SPAB's 40 cases no faculty had been sought, and in other cases it transpired that the 'destructive work' had been carried out by eminent architects such as G.F. Bodley, C. Hodgson Fowler, Sir Thomas Jackson and J.N. Comper. It is difficult to banish the thought that the Committee missed the point of the SPAB's criticisms – in the case of Comper's reredos at Burford, the Committee stated that 'it is denounced only because it was built into an ancient wall "instead of standing free"; ... the Committee cannot regard this as a very weighty indictment of the efficiency of the faculty jurisdiction'.[14] The SPAB had concluded by suggesting that it might undertake some official responsibility for the care and supervision of ancient churches, but the Committee pointed out that the SPAB had to realise two things: first, that churches were primarily place of worship, and, second, that it had expressed '[views] on the subjects of architectural science and antiquarian research which, however strongly held by some individuals, are not universally accepted'.[15]

The Committee recommended that the faculty jurisdiction should be improved and better publicised to churchwardens, and that 'an advisory body should be constituted in every diocese for the assistance of the court in architectural, archaeological, historical and artistic matters relating to churches as to which faculties are sought'.[16] Members of such committees should possess local knowledge and a range of experience, and should be unpaid. Diocesan committees would be necessary because

> in the opinion of the Committee a central body acting for all or many dioceses would not be advisable, not only because it would lack local knowledge but also because the amount of work thrown on the central body would be so great that it could not be expected to be undertaken by volunteers.[17]

In spite of the interruption caused by the First World War, which had broken out before the publication of the Dibdin Report, the matter was not forgotten. The interest of the church authorities was stirred by such cases as the sale of the fourteenth-century silver-gilt bowl and cover from Studley Royal church, Yorkshire. A faculty had been granted by the chancellor in January 1913 on condition that its sale, for £3,000, was restricted to the Victoria and Albert Museum. In 1915 Canon H.D. Rawnsley of Carlisle persuaded the House of Clergy of the Province of York to set up a committee to consider the Dibdin Report, and a resolution was passed urging that the proposed advisory committees should be consulted before, not after, reference to the chancellor.

Another factor which influenced the establishment of the advisory system was the natural desire of many individuals, families and parishes to commemorate those who had died in the Great War. The appalling losses, touching almost every family in the land, made it more than usually difficult to separate emotional demands from aesthetic principles. To avoid flooding churches with unsuitable or mass-produced tablets, the need for some control was recognised, and in October 1916 a pamphlet, *War Memorials*, was published by the Warham Guild which might have been a blueprint for an advisory system. It stated that:

The crux of the whole question is really that of an adequate survey of church buildings. The ideal seems to be that a list should be in existence for every church explaining in detail the things that are (1) virtually necessary for the stability and preservation of the structure, (2) desirable additions or alterations, and (3) harmless or allowable additions.

Under (1) may be classed the necessary renewal or strengthening of portions of the structure. Under (2) the substitution of suitable for incongruous necessary ornaments, such as the replacing of a bad altar and reredos by a good one, the erection of a good screen, the addition of a cover to the font, the replacing of plaster that has been wrongly stripped off walls or roof, the removal of thoroughly bad stained glass, and so on.

Under (3) would be included all that is purely decorative, and additional to the normal requirements of a church. Such things are – increasing a ring of bells, enlarging an organ, substituting a rich ornament for a plainer but otherwise satisfactory one, adding wallpaintings or stained glass, colouring a roof, and, above all, erecting what most people understand by the word 'monument'. It is in such things that the greatest danger lies, and in any given church all that is included under (1) and (2) ought to be exhausted before a donor is allowed to consider additions under (3).[18]

The author was Francis Carolus Eeles (FCE henceforth), a temporary civil servant cataloguing liturgical manuscripts and vestments at the V&A under Sir Cecil Harcourt Smith (1859–1944, Director and Secretary of the V&A 1909–24) who was a commanding figure with a great interest in church affairs; he was, for example, Chairman of the Court of the Incorporated Church Building Society. In those days there were few central bodies offering advice on artistic matters, and the Church was reluctant, following the debate on the Ancient Monuments legislation, to seek advice from the Ministry of Works. Thus many such inquiries came to the V&A, where they were increasingly passed to FCE. Discussions about the creation of an advisory system for protecting English churches and their treasures based on the Dibdin Report and arising from the pressure on the V&A's staff naturally followed. FCE had been involved in such discussions before, but now there seemed some chance of success. The idea became a reality at St Luke's Maidenhead on Whitsunday afternoon 1916 when the Bishop of Oxford (Charles Gore) told FCE that, following representations which FCE had made to him through Dr E.M. Blackie, Vicar of Windsor, he had decided to appoint an advisory committee, of which Harcourt Smith and FCE were to be members, to deal with war memorials, with the intention that it should in due course extend its reference to cover everything else.[19] In the event the first diocesan committee encompassing all aspects of churches and their contents was established in the Diocese of Truro, followed by Peterborough and Southwark. In April 1917 Harcourt Smith issued a circular on the care of church plate, and in 1919 the Museum put on an exhibition of war memorials in an attempt to raise standards. Meanwhile FCE continued to answer the growing number of inquiries on church subjects, which made it hard to concentrate on the cataloguing work for which he had been employed.

Matters now advanced more quickly: an informal meeting was held at the V&A on 28 June 1917 to encourage the formation of committees in other dioceses. A larger meeting on 14 March 1918 stressed the importance of comprehensive and accurate inventories of church property and proposed the formation of a central committee to assist diocesan committees if required. A third meeting later that year agreed that the diocesan committees should cover all aspects of churches and that the central committee should co-ordinate their work in order to achieve uniformity, to make available specialist advice on technical questions and to superintend the necessary survey work. In July 1920 the Ancient Monuments Advisory Committee of the Ministry of Works lent its support to the appointment of Diocesan Advisory Committees (DACs) as speedily as possible, and reiterated the threat that if cathedrals could not also be adequately protected they should be brought within the Ancient Monuments Act. By July 1921 a further informal meeting was told that, of the 37 dioceses then existing, 22 had a committee in existence or being formed, 8 were under consideration, and 2 had war memorial committees still in existence; in 1 case (Southwell) the bishop had refused to establish a committee, and in the remaining 4 no action had been taken. It was agreed that each diocese should send two delegates to a meeting in London, and it was this group which met in the Jerusalem Chamber on 4 November 1921.

For its part, the SPAB welcomed the formation of the Central Committee and of DACs, stating in its Annual Report for 1922 that

> This effort of the Church to set its house in order is worthy of all commendation and support. The Committee of the Society observes with satisfaction that the methods adopted are on the whole such as the Society approves; its relations with them have been uniformly friendly.[20]

So too, at a personal level, were the relations between A.R. Powys, the SPAB Secretary, and FCE, an SPAB Committee member, who exchanged many forthright but generally cordial letters over the ensuing years.

THE FOUNDING SECRETARY[21]

By good fortune FCE was the ideal person to take on the task of setting up the central committee to co-ordinate the work. In his late forties, he had a passionate interest in churches, their history, art and, above all, liturgy, while in many ways his life had prepared him for the task. The only drawback was that, as he had been a delicate only child, the constant wandering of his valetudinarian parents had deprived him of a normal childhood and schooling; instead, he had been taught by his father, and this solitary upbringing had left him rather shy and reserved in company. He could remember few childish playthings, and visits to churches soon became staple holiday pleasures. When he was 6 or 7 the family came to rest temporarily in the remote unspoilt West Somerset village of Porlock, where he developed a lifelong love of the West Country. A formative experience took place in Selworthy church in 1890 when FCE was 13. Watching workmen cutting away plaster from the quoins of the door to the rood stair he was shocked to see that in doing so they were destroying the border of a medieval mural painting. This, and the kindness of the architect and workmen at St Margaret, Lowestoft, Suffolk, who let the boy climb ladders to marvel at the intricate web of beams within the lead-covered spire, transformed his interest in churches from dry archaeological study into a determination to see churches and their treasures protected to safeguard their history, their beauty and, most importantly, their proper use – for worship. It was a determination emphasised by his later choice for a bookplate of an image of his patron saint, Saint Francis, surrounded by a scroll with the text of the Lord's command 'Francis, repair my house which is falling into ruin; beautify the place of my sanctuary, and I will make the place of my feet glorious.'

Later the family moved to Stonehaven, Kincardineshire, whence FCE

FIG 3 *Selworthy, Somerset, at about the time FCE first saw it. (Photograph in CCC collection.)*

went to tutors in Aberdeen with the intention that he should enter the university there. The daily train journey gave him a lasting enthusiasm for railways and trains; he was also developing interests in geology and church bells, and at the age of 19 gave his first lecture, published in 1897 as *The Church and Other Bells of Kincardineshire*. But his mathematical skills were not sufficient to pass the arithmetic examination required for matriculation, though in due course he attended some lectures as an external student. By now he was busy with liturgical and ecclesiological studies, and in 1899 he published a paper on *Reservation of the Eucharist in the Scottish Church*. In 1903 he was ordained (the term, of which he was proud, was used on his licence at the insistence of the bishop) reader in the Diocese of Aberdeen and Orkney.

FCE's father died in 1906, and in 1908 he married Mary Hall Wolfe, daughter of a Hungarian eye surgeon practising in Glasgow. They settled in Edinburgh, where his employment on research for a member of the Royal Commission on Historical Monuments for Scotland proved invaluable training for his later work. When the secretaryship of the Commission fell vacant in 1913 he applied for it, citing in his application the fact that he had visited most of the ancient churches in Scotland, as well as every church in London and Middlesex among other English counties (usually by train and bicycle, so his health must have improved at this period); but he was not appointed. Soon after he tried, again unsuccessfully, for the post of Assistant Inspector of Ancient Monuments in Scotland. But the climax of his years of Scottish ecclesiological study was the invitation in 1914 to give the Rhind Lectures to the Scottish Society of Antiquaries, of which he had been elected a Fellow in 1904. His subject was *The Liturgy and Ceremonial of the Mediaeval Church in Scotland*.

Perhaps partly as a result of his professional disappointments, FCE and his wife moved away to Keswick. Exempted on medical grounds from military service in the First World War, he pursued his ecclesiological interest amongst the local churches and at one point visited Crosthwaite church, Cumberland. Here he met the incumbent, Canon Hardwicke Drummond Rawnsley (1851–1920). A disciple of Ruskin at Oxford and later a friend of his in the Lake District, Rawnsley was a staunch defender of the nation's well-being, whether against the threat of defilement of the Cumbrian scenery by railway building, against the weakening of moral fibre from dubious literature available on station bookstalls or against the impairment of beautiful country churchyards by the introduction of white marble

FIG 4 *Dr Francis Carolus Eeles, OBE, D Litt, LL D, FSAScot, FRHistS (1877–1954). (Photograph in CCC collection.)*

headstones.[22] His ideals had found practical expression in 1895 when, with Octavia Hill and Sir Robert Hunter, he took part in founding the National Trust for Places of Historic Interest and Natural Beauty, of which he remained Secretary until his death. In spite of his interest in preservation, Rawnsley was amazed when FCE pointed out the condition of his own church and, in the wartime absence of professional architects, he asked FCE in 1915 to supervise extensive repairs to the church tower and bells, which added practical experience to his growing knowledge of the care and use of historic churches. Rawnsley also listened intently to FCE's proposals for an ecclesiastical advisory system, and urged the Bishop of Carlisle to form a committee. Although this did not come about at this stage, it was Rawnsley who was responsible for the motion passed by the House of Clergy of the Province of York which commended the Dibdin Report. He watched later developments with keen interest, but refused to become closely involved because of his National Trust commitments.

In about 1916 FCE and his wife returned to London to be with his mother, who from 1920 to 1932 was head of the Church Work Department at the Royal School of Needlework, carrying out designs by leading figures such as Comper and Christopher Webb for Westminster Abbey and many great churches. It was at this time that FCE joined the staff of the V&A under Sir Cecil Harcourt Smith to catalogue liturgical manuscripts and vestments, and it was logical that the office for the fledgling Council for the Protection of English Churches and their Treasures should be within the Museum, even though its secretary was often out of the office at site visits and committee meetings. His travelling must have been made easier when in 1923, under instruction from the church architect F.E. Howard, he obtained a driving licence.

FCE's complete identification of himself with the CCCC is evident not least from the fact that he worked for many years without a salary. With enormous enthusiasm for the work, he drove himself harder, in constant travelling about the country, attending meetings and writing reports, than his health could well stand. In 1948, for example, he paid 250 visits. By the end of his life he had seen the establishment of the Central Council and 42 DACs and had taken a warm interest in promoting advisory systems elsewhere including Scotland, Ireland, the USA and South Africa. In addition to his work for the Council, he served as reader successively in Aberdeen (where he attended St John's, the church where J.N. Comper's father had been rector), in Edinburgh (at Dr Blackie's church of St Paul, York Place), at St Mary Primrose Hill in the London years, and during the war at no fewer than 17 churches and chapels in West Somerset, while he also found time to be governor of two schools and to pursue his forward-looking interest in the ministry of women in the Church. In addition to the publications which he wrote for the CCCC he published 13 books and booklets, 18 church guides, contributions to 30 other books, 28 tracts and pamphlets, 25 editions of the *English Churchman's Kalendar*, about 50 articles for learned societies and over 40 descriptions of churches for the journals of the Somerset Archaeological Society. His achievements were recognised by an OBE and a Lambeth degree of Doctor of Letters, both conferred in 1937, and an Honorary Doctorate of Laws conferred by the University of St Andrews in 1951. He died aged 78 on 17 August 1954, the day before he was due to retire from the CCCC secretaryship because of ill-health. His ashes were buried in the churchyard at Selworthy, West Somerset, a church which he had cherished for over half a century. There he is commemorated by a stained glass window installed in the north aisle, designed by Christopher Webb and paid for by the CCCC. His topographical library forms the nucleus of the present CCC library; 2,000 of his books and his liturgical works and transcripts are deposited at Lambeth Palace Library; 400 books and his Scottish material are at Aberdeen University Library; and his CCCC papers are in the central archives of the Church of England.

2
The Central Council for the Care of Churches

EARLY DAYS

The clues to the character of the new Committee for the Protection of English Churches and their Treasures lie in the choice of the word 'protection' in the title, and they are twofold. The first, and more obvious, stems directly from the awakening of the conservation movement in England which had expressed itself in the anxieties about both over-restoration and neglect voiced by the SPAB, itself fighting under the banner of 'protection'. By the 1920s the SPAB had been joined by others. In the area of state legislation, the first Ancient Monuments Protection Act had been passed in 1882, revised in 1900, and replaced by the Ancient Monuments Consolidation and Amendment Act 1913, the debate on which had provoked the archbishops' undertaking to review the church system. In the realm of private enterprise, the National Trust had been founded in 1895, at first to protect endangered countryside, and had been given inalienable rights over its property by an Act of 1907. Following the premise that, in order to preserve, it is important to know what exists which may require preservation, the Royal Commission on Historical Monuments had been established by an Act of 1908 to compile inventories of the monuments in England surviving from the earliest times to 1700 (later extended on several occasions to more recent dates). Its first county report, on Hertfordshire, had been issued in 1910 and made it clear how much of the heritage was ecclesiastical. While the new Council was intended neither to take over possession of threatened churches nor to compile formal lists of what survives, its ultimate aim was the same as these two organisations – to preserve what has come down to us from the past.

The other clue is less obvious; it was the protection of the church furnishings and liturgical arrangements necessary for authentic Anglican worship. It is difficult for us in these ecumenical days, when our liturgies are all-embracing and frequently derive elements from other denominations, to realise what importance was attached to the Englishness of liturgical performance and arrangements a hundred years ago. The determination of the Oxford Movement to re-establish the Church of England as part of the God-given organisation known as the Catholic church had been largely achieved. But the Protestant elements within the Church were constantly critical of any aspect of outward ceremonial which could be labelled Papist. The advanced ritualists, seeking forms of worship and ceremonial which would conform with their theological outlook, had at first nowhere to turn for exemplars but to contemporary Roman Catholic practice. Peter Anson wrote,

> By the end of the last [19th] century, the furnishings and decorations of Anglo-Catholic churches were in a chaotic state. Most architects of the later Gothic Revival had either depended on their own imagination or had sought inspiration from contemporary continental sources, whether or not they were suitable for adaptation to the worship of the Book of Common Prayer. Few clergymen could claim much knowledge of liturgy.[1]

A sure defence against the critics lay, it was thought, in convincing them that each aspect of the ritual was permitted, indeed required, by the Book of Common Prayer and, especially, the 'Ornaments Rubric', which states that

> the chancels shall remain as they have done in times past, and here it is to be noted that such ornaments of the church, and of the Ministers thereof, at all times of their ministration, shall be retained and be in use as were in this Church of England, by the authority of Parliament, in the second year of the reign of King *Edward* the Sixth [1548–9]. [2]

That might seem fairly precise, but its exact interpretation was the source of endless debate which resulted in the establishment of several learned liturgical societies,[3] the principal of which were the Society of St Osmund, founded to encourage the revival of medieval ceremonial; the Henry Bradshaw Society (of which FCE was Secretary 1928–34), founded in 1890 to publish liturgical texts and service books with a bearing on the Prayer Book, and the Alcuin Club (of which FCE was Secretary 1903–10), founded in 1897 to promote the study of ceremonial and the proper arrangement of chancels in accordance with the ornaments rubric, and the only one which survives. Their overlapping membership included such scholars as Dr J. Wickham Legg, the Revd Dr F.E. Brightman, Cuthbert Atchley, Sir W.H. St John Hope and J.N. Comper.

   Although all these societies produced publications, their impact on parish churches was not great until the appearance on the scene of Percy Dearmer (1867–1936), a man of charisma and determination who perceived the need to put the message in an attractive package if it was to change the attitude of the parochial clergy. With this intention, he published in April 1899 the first edition of *The Parson's Handbook*. It was an immediate success, and ran through many editions but, in spite of the fact that Dearmer made it clear in the introduction[4] that he was doing no more than popularising the findings of others, several scholars resented it. Principal amongst his critics was J.N. Comper (1864–1960), the church architect, who prided himself on the fact that every aspect of the search for beauty which is evident in all his designs was based on his own meticulous research. He despised Dearmer, a liberal socialist, as a cheap populariser and plagiarist. But at that time Comper, although he had given his revolutionary theories physical reality in a number of church buildings and liturgical arrangements, had published only two obscure articles (the first, *The Gothic or English Altar*, appeared in the Transactions of the Aberdeen Ecclesiological Society in 1893 and was reprinted by the St Paul's Ecclesiological Society in 1895, and the second, *The Reasonableness of the Ornaments Rubric Illustrated by a Comparison of the German and English Altars*, was published in London in 1897. Neither is listed by Dearmer in the extensive bibliography in *The Parson's Handbook*.) Comper, throughout his exceptionally long life avoided publicity, hated any popularisation of his designs and continued to publish little. Dearmer, on the contrary, published widely, and while the reclusive Comper wrote in a precious, nebulous style in which 'his words wander by many dreamy paths into a kind of maze in which one never knows whether one has reached the centre or not', [5] Dearmer's prose was the work of a communicator – direct, persuasive and easy to follow.

On his visits and after his eventual return to London from Scotland in 1916, FCE lived in Hampstead and attended St Mary Primrose Hill, where Dearmer was putting his principles into practice with carefully ordered and dignified ceremonial in the English tradition accompanied by beautiful music (Martin Shaw was his organist), using vestments of correct shape and colour, and all set within spacious surroundings of whitened walls and richly coloured furnishings. FCE served as reader and, after Dearmer left for a canonry at Westminster Abbey in 1916, under Dr A.S. Duncan-Jones (later Dean of Chichester), as assistant parish clerk or sub-deacon at the Solemn Eucharist, until he left for Somerset at the outbreak of the Second World War. His admiration for Dearmer went far deeper than an appreciation of externals, for he endorsed Dearmer's insistence that however correct the worship and however uplifting the music, they were nothing without faith, a realisation which would underline all his own work for the CCCC.

When Dearmer left Primrose Hill, FCE gave a eulogy in which he asked the congregation:

> I wonder if you know how many people, men and women, many of them far away from St Mary's, sickened by the apathy of the Church to those social problems which cut down to the very roots of our life as a nation, have been saved to religion and to the Church by Dr Dearmer? And how many more attracted to the Church, who never thought that Christianity had any message for them? ... It is that wider Catholicism which has made St Mary's what it is.[6]

Having discovered that no established firms could produce the vestments required to conform with 'the English Use', in 1901 Dearmer launched the St Dunstan's Society. He soon realised that, in addition to vestments, properly designed furnishings and ornaments were required. In 1912, together with the Revd Jocelyn Perkins, Sacrist at Westminster Abbey, George Kruger Gray and FCE, and in alliance with the ecclesiastical furnishers A.R. Mowbray and Son, he formed a new organisation called the Warham Guild (after the last Archbishop of Canterbury before the Reformation), specifically to ensure 'the making of the ORNAMENTS of the CHURCH and the MINISTERS thereof according to the standard of the Ornaments Rubric and under fair conditions of labour',[7] with a showroom in Margaret Street. Comper's distrust of such commercial exploitation of the research carried out by himself and other scholars was reinforced when one of his pupils reported that he had seen in the Warham Guild window an altar and reredos which were in almost every detail a copy of Comper's work.[8] He was therefore critical when FCE, to whom he had earlier been a good friend, began to take a leading part in the establishment of Diocesan Advisory Committees and the Central Council, and he failed to understand the need for such a system if churches were not to be brought under state control, which would have affected him and his work, anti-preservationist as much of it was, more than some of his contemporaries.

An example of Comper's prose is the response[9] which he sent in 1924 to the Revd G.H. West, Secretary of the Gloucester DAC, who had written to Comper among others requesting examples of his work to illustrate a booklet of preferred designs for church furnishings. Although West's leaflet had explicitly stated that 'the use of trade catalogue or shop-made designs has been steadily discouraged in favour of the employment of artists who will make the work an expression of their own personality and in harmony with the building', Comper takes ten pages to deplore the growth of commercialism in church furnishings and, by extension, the influence of the new Diocesan Advisory Committees. This seems to have been about the time when he finally fell out with FCE, subsequently writing many petty things[10] against him and the advisory system.[11]

Another important vehicle for transmitting liturgical information to parishes was the *English Churchman's Kalendar*, published by Mowbray's, which gave on monthly sheets the lectionary and liturgical colour for each day of the year. In the remaining space was printed information about the care and arrangement of churches, vestments, liturgical ornaments and other kindred matters together with illustrations of commendable examples. From its foundation in 1895 until 1909 the *Kalendar*[12] had been edited by Dr J. Wickham Legg (1843–1921), a medical doctor who had given up practice in order to concentrate on liturgical studies, becoming the original authority of the late Victorian school of Anglican liturgiologists. Casting about for architects capable of transforming the results of his researches into stone and mortar, he first promoted J.T. Micklethwaite, the careful restorer of Inglesham church who as a young man, in his *Modern Parish Churches* (1874), had attacked pedantic antiquarianism, commercialism and 'go'[13] – by which he meant meretricious originality – and later became Surveyor to the Fabric of Westminster Abbey 1895–1906, and then the young J.N. Comper. During Legg's editorship, the *Kalendar* was a leading advertisement for Comper's work, but for the ten years[14] under Percy Dearmer nothing by Comper appeared, and for the years 1921–8 while it was edited by Dr E. Hermitage Day he only allowed occasional photographs of his work to be used.

The 1929 edition of the *Kalendar* appeared anonymously, prepared by the publishers, and from 1930, maintaining the anonymity, it was prepared by FCE. From this date the works of Comper never appear. Instead, the 1931 cover illustrates the work of Martin Travers; 1932 shows the reredos at Porlock by W. H. Randoll Blacking; 1933 the altar in the Regimental Chapel at Christ Church, Oxford, designed by H.S. Rogers; 1934 the south choir aisle altar at St Albans by Blacking. In subsequent years altars designed by F.E. Howard, Sir Walter Tapper and S.E. Dykes Bower were added to the list. FCE's breadth of interest ensured that these and medieval Gothic altars were complemented by examples of surviving Renaissance furnishings at places such as Staunton Harold, Derby Cathedral, St George Portland and Lydiard Tregoze, and by new churches both modern and traditional in style, such as St Saviour, Eltham (Cachemaille Day), St Thomas, Hanwell (Maufe), John Keble Church, Mill Hill (Martin-Smith) and All Saints, Hockerill (Dykes Bower).

Comper's scorn of those who imitated his work without having been through the process of research and discovery was exacerbated by FCE's powerful position as a patron of architects and designers, responding to parishes who approached him for suitable names. He seldom recommended Comper, not because he disapproved of his work, which he greatly admired, but because he knew him to be doctrinaire, difficult and expensive and also because his knowledge of liturgy and furnishings was not matched by structural expertise. 'I expect that, having had everything his own way at one time, he [Comper] did not trouble to relate his prices to present-day conditions',[15] the Archdeacon of Northumberland wrote to FCE in January 1935, and FCE replied frankly:

> I do not see what can be done to help him. He is so impossible. How can I or any of the rest of us recommend a man as an architect whose knowledge of construction is so deficient that his buildings are insecure? ... In years gone by I have done a great deal to help him in this way with little or no satisfactory result.[16]

FCE went on to deplore Comper's extravagance, his defiance of the liturgical authority of the Church of England and his continuing criticism of the advisory system. He pointed out that he had obtained at least £30,000 worth of work for Comper, including the Welsh National War Memorial in Cardiff, his only major secular work, and, with W.A. Forsyth, had saved him from a lawsuit over the collapse of his cross at Cirencester. He deeply regretted both Comper's enmity towards his own pupils and that although 'he is infinitely greater as an artist and as a designer than all the so-called great names of today, yet for some unaccountable reason he has become his own worst enemy'.[17] Only in very rare cases when FCE felt that a parish could cope with Comper's idiosyncrasies did he recommend him.

In other cases he tended to recommend Comper's pupils and disciples who would be more approachable. These included F.E. Howard, W.H. Randoll Blacking, W. Ellery Anderson, H.S. Rogers and Martin Travers. Thus while the only named architect in the CCCC's first report of 1923 was Comper, for his restoration of Rickmansworth parish church, later reports illustrate the work of these followers and the products of the Warham Guild, which executed designs for most of them. As has been pointed out, 'The reports make it quite clear that Eeles was promoting a style of church furnishing which he hoped would become the norm in the Church'.[18] This was not narrowly Gothic as Comper liked to imply. FCE's particular interest, formed as early as his time in Scotland, in the seventeenth century led to frequent commendation of Renaissance churches and their furnishings, which were mentioned in almost every CCCC report and illustrated in many *English Churchman's Kalendars*.

Nor would FCE recommend architects indiscriminately. In 1933 the son of one of his liturgiological friends wrote:

> When I started to practise some years ago you assured me that I need never be anxious about work as you would be able to recommend me for as much as I could carry out. I am writing to ask if you can recommend me for some now that things are so quiet ... I hear that something is to be done at Durham Cathedral, new altars etc., and some new churches ... in London. Can you do anything to push my name for some of these please?[19]

FCE responded briefly and coolly, 'I have frequently mentioned your name in connexion with work, and will do so again when circumstances are favourable. I have no influence whatever at Durham.'[20] Apart from architecture, the subject for which FCE was most often asked to recommend names was stained glass. An undated list in his handwriting of windows by J.C. Bewsey, for example, gives ten churches 'all the above due to me'[21] and then three more.

The estrangement between Comper and FCE lasted for a quarter of a century, during which FCE seldom responded to the criticisms which Comper put about. He did, however, give a lecture at Church House in late February 1934, in which he calmly answered point by point the criticisms which Comper had published in *Further Thoughts on the English Altar, or Practical Considerations on the Planning of a Modern Church* (1933). The story, however, ended in reconciliation, best expressed by a letter[22] from Comper's son and pupil Sebastian to FCE on 4 July 1949:

> I was very glad when yesterday my father showed me your learned book on the Scottish liturgy and told me that he was happily in touch with you again; I would like to add, if I may, my appreciation of your very generous attitude, for I am well aware of how naughty he has been.

In January 1950 Sebastian Comper wrote again, acknowledging FCE's contribution (which principally consisted of compiling a list[23] of Comper's work – no mean task) to the campaign organised by John Betjeman to obtain Comper a knighthood:

I have been prevented from writing to you earlier to express my very deep appreciation of the recognition conferred on my father, which I am sure must be primarily due to your very generous efforts. I use the word 'generous' because I am only too well aware of his past attitude in regard to the great work which you yourself have achieved. As you know, this attitude proceeded from not only impatience of any controls but from a strong conviction on grounds of principle, but I felt – in fact I think we all did – that he carried the matter much too far, and the long severance which followed was a matter of sad concern to me particularly.[24]

THE ESTABLISHMENT AND ORGANISATION OF THE CENTRAL COUNCIL FOR THE CARE OF CHURCHES

At first the CCPECT, composed of two representatives of each diocese, was an informal body which met twice, or sometimes only once, a year, with the casework being transacted by an Executive Committee of 20 members of whom FCE was one. A constitution was approved on 22 March 1923, and in the following year, when FCE officially became the first full-time Secretary, the Church Assembly included £500 in its annual budget. This allowed him to engage Canon Rawnsley's former secretary, Miss Minna Broatch, as his assistant. She served the Council for 17 years until 1940, when she retired back to Cumberland and became a member of the Carlisle DAC.[25]

In order to gain proper recognition for the Council's work amongst dioceses and parishes, it was important to bring it within the structure of the Church Assembly. This had been created in 1919 by the Church of England Assembly (Powers) Act which combined the two existing Convocations (houses of bishops and clergy) in each of the two provinces with a new house of laity to create a central legislative body and debating forum for the Church of England. A new constitution, formally establishing the Council as a board of the Church Assembly, was confirmed in 1927. Its full name was to be 'Central Council of Diocesan Advisory Committees for the Care of Churches' and its short title 'Central Faculties Council', but in the event the short title became 'Central Council for [the] Care of Churches'. The membership was to consist of two representatives from each DAC together with 15 members nominated by Church Assembly (of whom a minimum of ten were to be members of the Assembly), and there could be up to six further co-opted members, which resulted in a membership of over 100. The Chairman was to be chosen by the Council and approved by the Church

Assembly. Recognising the need to give equal attention to the two provinces, in 1923 the Central Committee had established separate committees to serve the Provinces of Canterbury and York, and matters were to be referred to the Central Committee by DACs only through them. By the summer of 1947 they were considered to have fulfilled their task and were dissolved. The Council continued to meet in the Jerusalem Chamber at the Abbey until 1958, when meetings were moved to Church House.

During the session of the Church Assembly on 13 June 1936, FCE was about in Church House to catch the ear of bishops about various matters. Seeing Guy H. Guillum Scott, QC, Assistant Secretary of Church Assembly and Chancellor of the Dioceses of Peterborough, Winchester and Oxford, he mentioned that he desperately needed an assistant to remain in the office during his many absences. Scott's immediate response was to offer the services of his daughter Judith (JDGS henceforth), who was reaching the end of her studies at the Byam Shaw School of Art in Kensington, and had shown an interest in architecture by attending some of Professor Richardson's lectures at University College, London. FCE saw her later that day and appointed her Honorary Assistant on the spot. She soon became Secretary of the Southern Provincial Committee, and on 12 February 1941 Assistant Secretary in succession to Miss Broatch.[26]

FIG 5 *FCE, JDGS and the two assistants in the main office at Dunster, photographed in October 1944 by James Nelson, one of the photographers who took a large number of photographs for the CCCC's national survey of churches. (Photograph in CCC collection.)*

The Council's office remained in the Victoria and Albert Museum until 1937, when the Director reclaimed the space because the International Congress on Art History would next meet in London. But the real reason for the Council's departure from the Museum was that the time had come for the Church to fund the Council's work since, so long as FCE remained on the staff of the V&A, both he and its office premises were being funded by the Government's Board of Education. The ultimate intention was to move the Council into Church House, Westminster, the headquarters of the Church Assembly, but, as that was in the middle of rebuilding, a five-year lease was taken on a temporary home at 123a Queens Gate, Kensington, SW7. To compensate for the loss of access to the V&A's library, FCE lent his collection of topographical books to the Council. But after only two years, war broke out in September 1939. FCE offered the Council the use of his house, Earlham, in Dunster, Somerset, which he had leased two years earlier. This was accepted with alacrity and, although rooms at Church House were allocated for the CCCC's use in 1945, its headquarters remained at Dunster for 16 years until 1955.

Finance was always very tight – at first FCE worked without remuneration other than bare expenses until in 1926 he was provided with an honorarium of £500 per annum which barely covered the expenses of his extensive travels; this arrangement lasted until 1947, when it was raised to £750 and called a salary. During the war years the Council occupied FCE's house in Dunster free of charge, and for the ten years thereafter the Central Board of Finance paid only the modest sum of £100 per annum towards rent, rates, heat and light. In 1940 it was reported that JDGS had worked full-time and unpaid for her first three and a half years; she then began to receive a salary of £150 per annum. In 1949 only 10 per cent of Council members claimed their travelling expenses and the most expensive DAC cost £40 to administer, which barely covered postage.

The seal was set on the advisory system by the passing of the Faculty Jurisdiction Measure in 1938 which established DACs as statutory bodies. The measure allowed minor repairs to be authorised not by a faculty, but by a certificate from the archdeacon, provided of course that the schedule of work had been approved by the DAC, an innovation which saved considerable time and expense. It also gave the archdeacon formal access to the consistory court, not only to apply for faculties for work which needed to be carried out but also to provide a sanction for illegal actions by allowing him to petition for the removal or remedy of unsatisfactory work at the expense of the perpetrator. The existence of the CCCC was only indirectly acknowledged; indeed, the sole mention of it was as the appointing body for two members of a rules committee. Nevertheless the rules which accompanied the measure enabled chancellors to refer matters directly to the CCCC for advice.

CHAIRMEN AND MEMBERS

The first Chairman, Bishop Herbert Edward Ryle,[27] Dean of Westminster, was an obvious choice. Born in 1856, a son of the first Bishop of Liverpool, he had been educated at Eton and King's College, Cambridge, of which he became a fellow for 20 years. His field was Old Testament studies and he had the reputation of being painstaking and accurate, with sound judgement, yet also an inspiring teacher. He was President of Queens' College from 1896 to 1900 and then successively Bishop of Exeter (1900–3) and Winchester (1904–11), becoming Dean of Westminster in 1911 for reasons of health. But his time at Westminster was not idle. Although his churchmanship was central (soon after arriving at Winchester he had dismayed the Anglo-Catholics by a pastoral letter forbidding certain ritualistic practices), he enhanced the dignity and beauty of the Abbey services with the constant support of Jocelyn Perkins, the learned Sacrist, and W.R. Lethaby, the Surveyor, who 'treated the fabric with great respect and studied it with intense care'.[28] An appeal which he launched in 1920 raised the enormous sum of £170,000 for maintenance of the building. Outside the Abbey he was a Prolocutor in Convocation, a member of many church committees and closely involved in the discussions about Prayer Book revision which dominated the 1920s.

When Ryle died in 1925 he was followed as Chairman by his successor as Dean of Westminster, William Foxley Norris,[29] who had been Vicar of Barnsley, Archdeacon of Halifax and then Dean of York for eight years. He has been described as 'a man of stately presence and forthright, perhaps slightly alarming, manner'[30] whose businesslike attitude did not always win results. He failed, for example, in his attempts to build a sacristy at the Abbey. None the less, his enjoyment of painting in watercolours and his reputation as a wise counsellor in artistic matters must have served him well as Chairman of the CCCC, which he remained for 12 years until his death in 1937, when he was succeeded by Dr D.H.S. Cranage, Dean of Norwich.

David Herbert Somerset Cranage[31] was born in 1866, and after private schooling also went up to King's College, Cambridge. Brought up in

Shropshire, he had devoted much of his early life to research on the churches of that county which gradually appeared in print as *An Architectural Account of the Churches of Shropshire* in ten volumes between 1894 and 1912, and has not been superseded. He was also that rare thing, a clergyman who had been made an Honorary Associate of the RIBA. Between 1902 and 1928 he was secretary of the Cambridge University Local Lectures, the forerunner of the Extra-Mural Department, and in 1928 he was appointed Dean of Norwich. He was 71 when he became Chairman of the CCCC and, after his resignation in 1953, he remained a member until his death in 1957 at the age of 91. His bishop said that 'he was urbane; there was a strong flavour of the eighteenth century about him ... he remained essentially a scholar though with great gifts as an administrator and organiser',[32] while W.I. Croome, his Vice-Chairman, wrote:

> Dr Cranage was a very great man, ... that exquisite courtesy, blended with uncommon shrewdness and firmness of purpose, with which he shut up a meandering bore, evaded any awkward question while seeming almost to purr with pleasure at having it asked, and quietly gaining his end almost without his opposition realising that he had done so, was indeed a lesson both in skill and urbanity.[33]

From the start the Council succeeded in attracting the services of many leading ecclesiastical figures of the day. During its first ten years alone, for example, the membership included: the liturgiologists Athelstan Riley and the Revd Dr E. Hermitage Day, the antiquaries the Revd G. Montagu Benton – at his death in 1960 the last survivor of the original Central Committee – and the Revd W.J. Pressey (who together compiled the magisterial inventory of Essex church plate), G. McNeil Rushforth (stained glass), Professor A. Hamilton Thompson (Church historian), F.H. Crossley (woodwork), H.B. Walters (bells), Sir Eric Maclagan (Harcourt Smith's successor as director of the V&A), and, amongst the architects, Sir Thomas Jackson, John Bilson, W.A. Forsyth, A.S. Dixon, Harold Brakspear, Sir Charles Nicholson, and P.B. Chatwin.

3
The work of the Council 1921–54

At the end of its first year, in December 1922, the CCPECT agenda included the proper treatment of bells, heating, churchyards, and the matter of derelict and disused churches. From the start it was clear that by its nature the Council's work would generally be re-active rather than pro-active. The first Annual Report, prefaced by a letter of commendation from the Archbishop of Canterbury (still Randall Davidson), was published in 1923. It gave an outline of the development of the system to date and made clear, in its condemnation of 'the vast amount of unnecessary destruction of ancient work of all periods'[1] which accompanied the Gothic Revival of the nineteenth century, that the Council's ideals would be in sympathy with those of the SPAB. Even at this early stage, moreover, attention was drawn to the importance attached to the Renaissance style. The Council continued to publish Reports every two or three years, the only illustrated reports produced by the Church Assembly.

By 1928 every diocese had a DAC, though Winchester and Portsmouth shared one until the War, and the CCCC noted with satisfaction that

There is a steadily increasing amount of interest in the history and care of our churches in many parts of the country, which is very largely due to the Diocesan Committees. It is now the exception in most districts to find a parish church which is not open every day. In many cases leaflets or booklets are available, giving an outline of the church and its architecture. Fabrics and their contents are better kept ... there are frequent cases where valuable possessions have been recovered after long disuse or alienation. The problem of disused and ruinous churches and chapels is being faced.[2]

By the time of the sixth Report, covering 1932–3 (again with the imprimatur of a preface by the Archbishop of Canterbury, now Cosmo Gordon Lang), the Advisory Committee system involved 350 people in the dioceses and 98 in the central council and two provincial committees, all giving their time and talents free of charge.

A summary was published under the headings 'What the System has

Done', 'What the System has NOT Done', 'What the System CANNOT do' and 'What the system ought not to do'. The positive points still inform the system today – stimulation of interest in churches, ensuring more conservative and scientific standards of repair, preserving ancient work from destruction, restoring ancient and valuable fittings which had been alienated or disused, clearing churches of 'valueless obstructions', checking the increase of tablets on walls and inferior stained glass windows, saving bells from needless recasting, ensuring the proper treatment and placing of organs, raising the standards of modern work, 'checking the Victorian claim that the artist or architect of today has a right to leave his own impression on an ancient building or to obscure or alter it', opening doors to freshness and experiment where new churches are concerned, and being alive to the danger of passing fashions. The Report admitted, however, that the system had not yet 'established itself with efficiency or regularity of working in certain areas in the country', it had not always avoided minor mistakes and it had not always been able to 'overcome ignorance or hostility or the ingrained bad customs of a century that prided itself on the "Gothic revival"'. What the system could not do was to allow or forbid any work in a church – only the chancellor could do that; nor could it interfere with the judicial process of the consistory court, nor grant any money 'because it has not got any', nor 'make a bad architect into a good one or redraw his designs'. Substantial alterations should not be proposed to designs on which an artist or architect of high repute had spent much time and trouble, without very good reason. Criticisms should be phrased as suggestions respecting artists' feelings. Above all, it ought not to cause delay nor give the slightest cause for suspicion that some artists are being unduly favoured at the expense of others.[3]

Much of the Council's time was naturally taken up with discussions about relationship with DACs. Although the Council had been charged with the duty of correlating the work of DACs, it could in no sense be considered a governing body, and DACs staunchly maintained their independence. Indeed, in 1926 it had been noted that, while DACs were appointed by the bishop, the Central Committee was no more than a voluntary organisation (it received its constitution in the next year). It was agreed in 1927 that the minutes of all DACs should be sent to the central office (although it seems unlikely that this happened in every case until many years later). More than once the presence of architects and artists on DACs was questioned. The CCCC's practical line was that they could contribute much and should not be debarred, but that they should leave the room for discussions or votes on their own work. One of the most important ways in which the Council assisted the work of DACs was by publishing booklets and pamphlets on a wide range of subjects, a list of which is given in Appendix 2. The last survivor of the original DAC Secretaries was H.E. Singleton Turner, of St Edmundsbury and Ipswich, who died in 1950. Thus FCE outlived all the first generation of DAC Secretaries.

CHURCH FURNISHINGS

Alongside its attention to church buildings, the Council was keen to promote responsible attitudes towards the care of existing furnishings and the quality of new introductions. Church bells, for example, a subject in which FCE had a particular interest, occupied its time throughout the period; a memorandum on bells was published in the first Report, and others followed over the years. By 1932 H.B. Walters had prepared diocesan schedules of bells of historic interest, which were sent to each DAC. In the 1930s and 1940s 'radio bells' were condemned on several occasions. An interdict on the ringing of church bells during the Second World War led to neglect of maintenance which had to be remedied afterwards. In 1949 a proposal to recast the thirteenth-century bell at Crosby Garrett, Westmorland, one of the oldest bells in the north of England, was met with horror.

The Council's interest in church plate was stimulated by a proposal in 1929 to sell a sixteenth-century cup from St Mary, Sandwich, and a CCCC report on the sale of church plate was published in 1933. Nevertheless, in 1948 and 1949 there were two examples of faculties for the sale of plate (a pair of Charles II flagons from Kenn, Devon and a Charles I flagon from Lingfield, Surrey) without the Council being consulted. In the former case the DAC had advised strongly against sale, and in the latter the DAC had not even been consulted. The reason given in both cases, that the flagons were secular pieces, was considered by the Council to be unfounded.

Stained glass, another field of special interest to FCE, first came to the Council's attention in 1925, when the urgency of recording medieval glass was noted, but the financial difficulties were thought to be insuperable. Likewise, a committee for stained glass and wallpaintings established in the following year seems to have achieved little. In 1930 the British Society of Master Glass Painters, of which Sir Cecil Harcourt Smith was Chairman, complained about DACs causing delay and treating their members unfairly, but they were kindly met by the Dean of Westminster (who as Dean of York had raised £50,000 for the conservation of the Minster glass) and good relations were established which FCE took care to maintain, not least by writing explanatory articles for their Journal in 1944 and 1950–1. After the war, FCE noted that much bad glass was being retained in war damage repairs, instead of being eliminated or modified to achieve more light. He was not, however, condemning Victorian glass out of hand, for he had written that 'it is now fully recognised that a very great deal of the glass of the Victorian period is extremely fine in character and well worthy of preservation',[4] instancing especially the sad loss in the war of the Clayton & Bell glass at St John, Red Lion Square, and the early Kempe glass at St Agnes, Kennington.

On the practical matters of heating and lighting, the Council published guidance on several occasions, as will be found in Appendix 2. In 1931 doubts were expressed about gas lighting, in 1934 it was recommended that brass chandeliers should not be wired for electricity, and in 1948 the Council discouraged the use of fluorescent lighting, although it 'might be experimented with in a church in Renaissance style or a simple modern building'. Flood lighting (inside churches) was also disliked, especially when it was installed in Holy Sepulchre Northampton in 1949 without consultation with the Peterborough DAC. In 1953 the Council published two sheets of recommended designs for electric light fittings, prepared in conjunction with the National Association of Church Furnishers.

A minor type of furnishing, in more ways than one, was the children's corner, consisting of miniature chairs and tables and sentimental prints of the childhood of Christ after Margaret W. Tarrant, which became fashionable in the early 1930s. The CCCC felt that there was nothing to be said in their favour, either on grounds of aesthetics or theology, since if children came to church they should either remain with their parents or be taught in a Sunday School. One member wondered who was expected to celebrate at a 2ft high altar. By 1945 it was reported that the circulation of a memorandum by the Gloucester DAC had 'already been the means of checking the spread of these corners', but a further publication was required in 1954.

One example, among many, must suffice of the CCCC's interest in unfashionable and neglected categories of furnishing in churches. In 1930 it published a report pleading for the retention of box pews:

the time seems to have come to call a halt to the modernisation of what has now become a small group of churches, most of which are in sparsely populated localities. For the sake of historic interest, and picturesque if not always artistic values, such interiors ought to be retained as far as possible intact.[5]

CHURCHYARDS

Like bells, churchyards were the subject of early discussions and a leaflet, *Care of Churchyards*, later to grow into the *Churchyards Handbook*, was issued in 1930. In 1932 controversy ensued when a chancellor granted a faculty for a white marble headstone, and in the following year Guy Dawber and Gilbert Ledward set up a scheme under the chairmanship of Dean Foxley Norris, the CCCC Chairman, for supplying well-designed churchyard monuments at modest cost. They published a book of examples in 1938.[6] In 1935 the CCCC opposed the scheduling of churchyard monuments as ancient monuments by the Ancient Monuments Board as contrary to the spirit of the Dibdin Report, and this opposition was reiterated in 1938 when the Board proposed to schedule the Bewcastle cross. The Board proceeded with scheduling nevertheless, and asked local archaeological societies to prepare lists of monuments earlier than 1600. The CCCC could only protest again that this was unduly aggressive and contrary to the spirit of the agreement offered by Archbishop Davidson. In 1941 the CCCC was asked by the parish of Hampton, Middlesex, for a view about growing vegetables in churchyards to help the War effort, but decided that this was not a matter on which action should be taken.

GRANTS AND SYSTEMATIC CARE

The Council's work was transformed in the mid-1930s by an approach from the Pilgrim Trust, a major grant-giving organisation founded in 1930 with large funds at its disposal and more liberal terms of reference than most charitable trusts. Having given generously to church repair from the outset, the Trust from 1934 specifically sought FCE's advice on church applications, and in addition gave him £200 per annum to allocate at his own discretion towards the preservation of church treasures.[7] By 1947 the Trust had allocated a total of £153,000 towards church and cathedral repairs. In 1951 all Pilgrim Trust grants were suspended for a time 'pending the evolution by the Church of England of a scheme for providing more methodically for the maintenance of this priceless series of buildings'[8] but, once the systematic inspection of churches was in place, funding resumed in a revised form. From 1954 the Pilgrim Trust awarded an annual block grant for church fabric repairs to the newly established Historic Churches Preservation Trust (HCPT) and provided the CCCC with an equivalent sum to allocate towards the conservation of church contents.

The matter of regular inspection of churches was not new to the Council. From the beginning it had commended the SPAB's strategy of 'staving off decay by daily care' in place of a cycle of gradual decay and major restoration every few decades. In 1937 Sir Cecil Harcourt Smith had drawn attention to the need for the systematic inspection of churches. The problem was that many existing diocesan surveyors, appointed by the bishops, were still rooted in the tradition of periodic drastic restorations, and would not be temperamentally suited for such work, while it would be too much for archdeacons to organise. For 14 years nothing was done, but in 1951 a Commission including among its membership three CCCC representatives, the Dean of York, the Archdeacon of Wisbech and Mr Laurence King, was set up by the Church Assembly. In the next year it reported that 'in the past thirty years the Church has carried through a vast amount of repair on sounder and more conservative lines than ever before';[9] that 'the primary cause for the present state of disrepair of many churches is the enforced postponement of repairs during the ten years from 1939 onwards owing to the difficulty of obtaining labour, raw materials and licences';[10] and that 'the amount of extra-parochial aid needed to supplement the efforts of parishes in putting their churches into a state of good repair over a period of ten years is estimated to be £4,000,000',[11] with the prospect of annual expenditure thereafter of £750,000.

Various ways of raising the money were proposed, including the introduction of state aid alongside secular historic buildings, tax incentives and, most importantly, the establishment of a 'Trust for the Preservation of Historic Churches', with subsidiary county trusts, to raise the £4 million by national appeal. The report also commended the advisory committee system and several initiatives which the CCCC had long been promoting, especially the inclusion of lectures on the care of churches in courses at theological colleges, the issue of an explanatory leaflet to incumbents and churchwardens, and the regular quinquennial inspection of every church by a suitably qualified architect, with subsequent repairs being carried out under similarly expert supervision. It recognised that training in traditional building methods would be required to establish a supply of such architects.

This was a subject which the CCCC was particularly anxious to promote, and in 1953 FCE established that courses were being run by the SPAB, the Bartlett School of Architecture in London University and the University Development Trust at York.

In May 1952 Ivor Bulmer-Thomas, who had chaired the Commission, attended the CCCC to explain the proposal for forming a new trust to offer grant aid when parishes could not meet their repair costs. In 1954 the HCPT was established, and amongst its distinguished trustees, including the two Archbishops, the Lord Chancellor, the Prime Minister, the Leader of the Opposition and the Speaker, were the Dean of York and Will Croome (the CCCC's Vice-Chairmen), while FCE and JDGS were members of an informal Advisory Panel.[12]

SOME EARLY CASEWORK

A major psychological problem which the Council and DACs had to overcome was the distrust of interfering central authorities felt by many parishes. This was understandable; the parish church remained, and remains, in the freehold of the parson, with its contents vested in the churchwardens. Since 1921 the parochial church council had been charged with the duty, previously laid on the churchwardens, of obtaining funds for the care, maintenance, preservation and insurance of the parish church.[13] The monitoring of church fabrics was, and is, the responsibility of the bishops, exercised by their archdeacons, and there was a reluctance to accept a new tier of control. This attitude was also a prime cause for the parlous state of a small number of churches. Some notable early cases in which the Council became involved through its secretary indicate the concerns of the time, in particular the CCCC's determination to educate parishes and architects in the best methods and materials for the repair of churches, to encourage alienated furnishings to be returned to use, and to promote the introduction of new work of good quality. All this was underpinned, in the days before state aid for churches, by grant aid provided by the Pilgrim Trust.

In view of his long experience of the churches of the South West, FCE did his best to ensure that they could be held up as examples of architectural care and liturgical excellence to be followed throughout the rest of the country. It therefore caused him particular pain when something went wrong there. Broadhembury[14] is a typical Devon church with particularly good waggon roofs in the nave and south aisle, the former with an enriched section over the site of the rood just in front of the chancel arch. In 1929 the roofs, which were showing signs of damp, were stripped of plaster by the diocesan architect, Mr Harbottle Reed, 'to facilitate examination'. It was found that the common rafters were painted with a running foliage pattern on a red ground. FCE was asked to inspect and report; he did so on 18 November 1929, and said that he was 'amazed at the interest and beauty of what was revealed'. The painted decoration was 'of an extraordinary richness, unmatched anywhere else in my experience – and I think it is quite possible that I have seen more west of England roofs than anyone else'. FCE urged 'the necessity of taking every possible precaution to ensure the preservation of this wonderful treasure of Devonshire art', and advised Mr Harbottle Reed to meet Mr P.M. Johnston, 'a distinguished authority on the preservation of ancient colour work'.

But the next FCE knew was that, although Harbottle Reed had consulted Johnston, he had removed all the painted timbers from the roof; those from the south aisle were sold for firewood for £75, and those from the nave left in a heap in the churchyard. Johnston visited again and found the wood in the churchyard to be seriously infected and unusable. He formed a poor view of the men working for Dart & Francis, the contractors, 'one of whom was too ready to quote the training he had received from Victorian architects of distinction in modern work who were very destructive where old work was concerned'. When FCE visited again, he was 'horrified at the change in the appearance of the nave roof – I could only distinguish some six or seven of the painted rafters'. Some painted ribs were roughly set aside in a corner, and delicate painted bosses and cresting from the enriched part of the roof were piled behind the organ. The vicar, whom FCE had not previously met, tried to make amends by offering him three pairs of painted rafters for the V&A and the Taunton Museum. Where was the pile said to be in the churchyard? Eventually, after some prevarication on the part of the vicar, it was revealed that the contractors had urged the PCC to have it burnt, so it had been sold to Mr Bowles, who needed firewood urgently, for 10/-. The next day FCE visited his cottage 'in a remote part of the parish in a place only accessible by a rough narrow lane with a deep ditch on one side' expecting to find rotten rafters. There were in fact two stacks of very sound oak with lengths of moulding, some still coloured, much of which could have been re-used. The rotten rafters had been taken elsewhere, and FCE was told that he was too late to see them. Realising that the wood could not now be replaced in the church but was likely to be burnt as firewood, FCE bought it from Mr Bowles and had it removed to store in Somerset, perhaps to be put back in Broadhembury church in the future.

The opportunity came sooner than expected, with the Pilgrim Trust's approach to the CCC in 1934 to assist with the allocation of church grants. Broadhembury received the first large grant (£400), the work being done under the supervision of Professor A.E. Richardson. But the case had caused FCE extreme anxiety about the public credibility of the advisory system. Although he was forgiving enough to help the parish to draft an appeal leaflet, he wrote to the PCC Secretary that

> whatever you do, do not approach the Society for the Protection of Ancient Buildings or send any appeal to any of its members. This is vital. If an appeal reaches any of their members they will be almost certain to come down and examine the church and try to obtain information. We shall then be accused of what I am afraid is the fact, viz. trying to cover up a scandal.

FCE had no doubt where the blame lay, for he wrote to Sir Cecil Harcourt Smith, 'As you know, things are very bad in Exeter and I have to take endless trouble in order to make the machine work at all in that diocese; it is partly the fault of Sir Francis Newbolt, the chancellor, partly the Registrar and chief officials.'

The business at Porlock,[15] a church which FCE had known intimately from childhood, touched on several aspects of his life. As early as 1909 he had been entrusted by the Synod of the Diocese of Aberdeen with setting up a memorial to Adam Bellenden, Bishop of Aberdeen from 1635 to 1638 who, after being extruded from his diocese, became rector of Porlock until his death in 1647. There is no indication of his burial at Porlock, and the Synod felt that 'a small and perfectly plain brass or bronze tablet would be quite enough'.[16] On 10 February 1930 the annual vestry commended a suggestion that the east end of the church should be improved, and FCE saw his chance. A reredos incorporating a painted figure of Bellenden and his arms was designed by W.H. Randoll Blacking, described by FCE as 'about the best of the younger men', with painted figures by Christopher Webb, in a style which had 'a Gothic flavour but was not a copy, having neither a cusp nor a crocket anywhere'.[17] The rector, the Revd Derman Christopherson, tried to play down the Scottish connection, feeling that FCE had appropriated a parish project to achieve his own ends and that local donors would be offended. But the reredos was installed as designed, and when in due course it was dedicated on 19 April 1931 the Chancellor of Aberdeen University was present. It appeared on the cover of the *English Churchman's Kalendar* for 1932.[18]

Early in 1933 Blacking reported on the state of the tower with its unusual truncated spire. His report was approved by the SPAB, FCE calling it 'a peculiarly deserving case', the funds were found and by January 1934 work was complete. However, Blacking was accused of over-charging – on a total

FIG 6 *The Porlock reredos designed by W.H. Randoll Blacking and painted by Christopher Webb, with the figure of Bishop Bellenden in the right-hand panel. (Photograph in CCC collection.)*

cost of £528 1s 4d he charged fees of £62 18s and expenses of £15 16s 9d (for six visits) – and was dismissed. It turned out that the dispute was really between the two churchwardens, both rival local builders. One had done the work on the spire, which disgruntled the other, who was therefore allowed to carry out the next piece of work, the repair of the porch. What he did proved to be 'of a very damaging character' which 'destroyed old work and put in brand new stonework in the forefront of this exceedingly picturesque old building'. The SPAB found out and asked their Secretary, A.R. Powys, to investigate. The chancellor told FCE that Porlock must apply for a faculty, and the archdeacon said that the DAC was only advisory and had no authority other than moral. Powys visited with Philip Sturdy, a member of the DAC, on 3 March 1934 and inspected the rebuilt buttress. They reported that the builder/churchwarden was proud of his church and of his work and that the parish, feeling 'sufficient unto itself' in ordering its affairs, had decided that no faculty was needed (with which Powys and Sturdy did not agree). Their assessment of the new buttress encapsulated the real problem. It was built

> of excellent stone laid in too hard and impervious mortar; the mason work is in the very best present-day tradition, and it has about it no trace of the revival of traditions which were existent when medieval masons worked ... but from the point of view of archaeology, of romance, of sentiment, of antiquity, of beauty and of economy, a mistake has been made.[19]

Further, 'the new buttress appears conspicuous, hard and unkind; the remaining one mellow, gentle and modest'.[20] They described the proper treatment for the remaining old buttress and suggested that the new buttress might best be toned in by being limewashed with the rest of the church. A few months later W.D. Caröe, who was unfortunately both a bitter opponent of Blacking and no friend of the SPAB, was appointed to supervise future work. Nevertheless, Blacking courteously wrote to him,

> When passing the church a few months ago I noticed that a particularly unfortunate piece of 'restoration' work was being carried out without, I believe, the advice of an architect, so I am glad to know that you have been called in and that the building will be once more in the hands of an architect.[21]

Two cases concerning screens show the excitement aroused by the restoration of displaced furnishings, and the care which FCE took to ensure that all the parties involved – usually the parish, the architect, the DAC,

FIG 7 *The screen from St Audries, photographed in the workshops of Messrs A.R. Mowbray before being erected in Exford Church, showing clearly the repairs and additions.* (*Photograph in CCC collection.*)

the SPAB and the CCCC – were kept well informed and satisfied about the methods used. In West Somerset the early sixteenth-century screen of St Audries or West Quantoxhead church, had lain in pieces ever since the church had been rebuilt to a different design in 1858. Early this century it had been discovered and published by Bligh Bond, who drew attention to its importance as one of a group centred on Dunster, others of which survive in half a dozen churches in the neighbourhood. As a result the pieces had been removed to be stored in the V&A. It could no longer be re-erected at St Audries, so in 1912 it was offered to Williton church, and in 1925 to Selworthy, but both proposals fell through. Nothing further happened until 1928 when FCE offered it to Exford[22] church and it was accepted by the PCC. The work was carried out by Messrs A.R. Mowbray under the direction of Blacking with advice from the Bath & Wells DAC, F.E. Howard and FCE. The 200 surviving pieces were fitted together, new parts, including the whole framework and the sill, were made, and half a bay was added at each end. No conjectural restoration of loft, cresting or bosses was undertaken, and the extensions to the vine trail cornice were left uncarved. The outer panels below the dado had apparently never had tracery, and the new ones were therefore left plain. When later paint was cleaned off, it became clear that the screen had never been coloured. It was erected in the church together with a sympathetic new pulpit designed by Blacking in place of a mid-nineteenth-century stone one. The completed work was dedicated by the Bishop of Taunton on 6 October 1929, when FCE gave an address about the history of the church and screen. Three weeks later Mr Squires of Mowbrays responded to a congratulatory letter from FCE by admitting that,

> It was a somewhat difficult and tedious job, e.g. it was a temptation to the staff when to have made an entirely new detail would have been easier and quicker than to joint and patch an old piece! But in the end your and Mr Blacking's instructions and wishes were carried out in the letter and the spirit.

So important did FCE consider Exford as an example of what could be done that he persuaded the Church Assembly to publish a pamphlet for the encouragement of others, apparently the only time they had done such a thing.

The other screen was the magnificent example at Attleborough[23], Norfolk, dating from the third quarter of the fifteenth century with heraldic painting of c.1615. It had been threatened with destruction in 1842 but had been saved by the intervention of Professor Willis, even though three years later the parish ignored his advice not to move it from its original position and placed it at the west end of the church. There it had stood ever since, with much of its colour covered with white paint. A joint report by F.E. Howard and Professor Tristram in 1930 recommended that it should be reinstated across the east wall of nave and aisles, with some missing parts replaced and the whole painted surface cleaned and restored. In March 1930 the CCCC encouraged

> the possibility of its being treated for repair and preservation in the most modern scientific manner and being displayed to its best advantage in a way worthy of one of the greatest artistic treasures in the country ... the [CCCC's Southern Provincial] Committee considers it essential that the screen should be replaced in its original position.

In the discussions which followed about the precise extent and style of the replacement of missing parts, and the technical methods of keeping the sill away from damp and preserving the coloured decoration, FCE played a leading and characteristically irenic role so that, in spite of some rough passages with F.E. Howard and the SPAB, the work was eventually carried out to the satisfaction of all parties.

In 1937 the Vicar of Bridgwater[24] sought advice on the interior of the

FIG 8 A & B *The Attleborough screen, shown at the west end of the church in an old postcard, and as re-erected across the east end of nave and aisles, when the remains of the painted rood and attendant figures were found on the wall above.(Photograph in CCC collection.)*

town's fine medieval parish church. It was the first major case which JDGS visited on her own. Her draft report which advocated replastering the nave walls and limewashing all the walls, replacing a nineteenth-century tiled floor with stone slabs, and rearranging the sanctuary with an English altar, must have confirmed FCE's decision that she was the right person to assist

FIG 9 A & B *St Columba, Haggerston, before and after the whitening advocated by the CCCC. (Photographs by Gordon Barnes in CCC collection.)*

him in the future. 'I have just scribbled a few notes after returning from Portsmouth in haste: this report is *first rate*; you have only to write it out in full and send it to [the vicar]' he wrote across the top and told the vicar,

I am in entire agreement with all she suggests; she seems to have thoroughly understood the situation and although I will make a point of coming to Bridgwater as soon as I can get to the West of England, I do not think there is anything that I should like to put differently.

The whitening of interior walls, and the exterior walls where historically appropriate, was a basic tenet of FCE's, and one which he had probably learnt from Comper, who wrote of

> the custom which has obtained right through the ages of painting white or limewashing the whole interior of the church ... in England we have scraped practically every church to its immense loss and we have, I fear, set a bad example elsewhere.[25]

The purpose was to obtain light, increase the apparent scale of the building, to make a restful background for coloured furnishings and fittings and, above all, to make it uniform so that the eye would not be caught by irregularities in the structure. In the 7th Report (1937), under the heading 'The "Yellow Peril"' FCE stressed the importance of using pure white, 'not yellow or cream or stone colour ... there are even worse cases where grey or blue or some dark colour has been used'.

Following the example of St Mary, Primrose Hill, where Dearmer had whitened the interior of a brick-faced Victorian church, FCE recommended whitening for all Victorian churches. He therefore wrote in 1939 of St Columba, Haggerston, where the internal wall surfaces are likewise of exposed red brick,

> this is considered one of the finest 19th-century churches in London. It is perhaps the finest work of James Brooks, who was among the very outstanding architects of his time. The proportions are magnificent, even though the interior was left bare of the decorative treatment Brooks intended. By far the greatest need of the building today is that the interior should be whitened. Only in this way can the beauty of its architecture be seen and appreciated. It is almost impossible without great expenditure of money to get the walls and stonework back to their original appearance, and even if that could be achieved there would still be the unsatisfactory dark red walls.

His justification for what today seems debatable advice was that,

> It is very important that it should be understood that it was only a passing fashion of the Victorian era to leave inside walls bare. No-one ever left exposed red brick walls inside a church before that time and nobody does it now. White was the groundwork of interior wall treatments all down the ages ... so it is not a mere personal preference or idiosyncrasy.

The last major case illustrates the debate between conservation and improvement, as topical in the 1990s as in the 1930s, and concerns the Suffolk church of Ufford[26] with its magnificent font and cover, about which the incumbent asked Comper's advice in 1934. The DAC felt that for once Comper was a restraining influence on the rector's enthusiasm for improvement, but noted that he favoured the removal of the font from its place near the entrance. The DAC asked the advice of the SPAB. FCE wrote a warning letter, pointing out Comper's hate of criticism, his distrust of the advisory system and his dislike of the SPAB, adding that he believed that Comper wanted to 'do too much' to the font cover, making

a complete restoration on lines which nowadays would be considered inadmissible, I should think, by every Advisory Committee in the country and almost certainly by the Central Council if this case were to come before it ... I have no doubt that Mr Comper would carry it out well, and there may be a few people who would feel that they would like to see one of those great font covers made to look exactly as it must have looked of old. I cannot see that this could be done without involving that conjectural restoration which the Central Council has emphatically condemned ... today it is essential that nothing should be done to what is after all a great national treasure that would not secure universal approval or that would stimulate agitation against the system set up by the Church.

He was also worried that the contractors 'although they do excellent work under competent supervision, are regarded as exceedingly thorough and drastic, and a combination of this architect and these contractors uncontrolled would certainly not command the confidence of those best qualified to speak on the matter'.

Comper replied that he had always felt unable to recognise the assumption by DACs of authority to give rulings in matters of taste, even though 'I most fully recognise and welcome the exercise of the purpose for which, as I believe, the Committees were instituted, viz., to protect our ancient fabrics and ornaments'. The DAC had apparently endorsed his report with one exception, and he objected to interference in five 'points of detail which properly lie within the province of the architect'. Three people, W.A. Forsyth, H.M. Cautley and FCE, provided written observations on Comper's letter. FCE suggested that the DAC should oppose the removal of the font cover from the church to Cambridge for repair, that any move of the font should only be to its original position, centrally and raised up at the west end of the church, but that in the absence of exact knowledge it should remain more or less where it was, and that the conjectural restoration of ancient colour to the cover should be opposed. A note that the DAC endorsed these points closes the file, and the

Fig 10 *Gipping Chapel, Suffolk, before and after the re-arrangement, repair and re-leading of the stained glass with the advice of the CCCC. (Photographs* East Anglian Daily Times *and* Slide House Ltd, *in CCC collection.)*

font remains in the same position today, with its cover uncoloured.

FCE's advice was also sought on less typical matters. The first concerned a 'peculiar', that is to say a church which falls outside the normal jurisdiction. It was the extra-parochial chapel at Gipping,[27] Suffolk, a building with good late medieval glass, which was vested in trustees. The Revd E.G. Falconer, vicar of the neighbouring parish of Old Newton, had been curate of the chapel since 1890 and, disagreeing with his trustees that the chapel needed repair, refused to let a delegation consisting of the archdeacon (chairman of the trustees), rural dean and FCE to enter it in 1935. Later the situation became almost farcical, when the trustees instructed Misses Townshend & Howson to remove the glass to London. On the day their workmen arrived, they were turned out of the chapel, the door was locked behind them, and they were driven to Stowmarket station by Falconer's son and put on a train back to London. The men were anxious because they had already loosened much of the glass but had not taken it out of the window. FCE wrote to the archdeacon that

if anything goes wrong with the glass it will be the equivalent of vandalism such as went on in East Anglia in the 17th century; under these circumstances I shall not fail to make a public exposure of this man Faulkener [sic], and will do my best to see that his name will go down to posterity with that of the notorious William Dowsing.

In the end the Court of Chancery found in favour of the trustees, and the re-arrangement and re-leading of the glass in the east window was carried out in 1938 with the help of a Pilgrim Trust grant of £50 awarded through the CCCC.

The other matter was referred by the Bishop of Chelmsford.

The *Essex Free Press* of 16 February 1933 reported 'The usually placid life of the parish of Middleton has been disturbed this week by the intrusion of many strangers intent upon gleaning first-hand information regarding a series of remarkable claims made by the Rector and his organist, supported by some other personages. Nothing quite like it has occurred anywhere in this country for many a long day. In short it is that the Blessed Virgin Mary has appeared in the Rectory grounds and church, whilst a boy has had dreams concerning the church, as a result of which interesting archaeological and historical discoveries have been made.' [28]

On the Sunday night, during evensong 'at which incense was freely used, so much so in fact that one lady had to hurriedly seek the porch and another young lady, just before the sermon, had to be assisted out', the rector had preached a sermon saying that on the previous Sunday he had seen the Crucifixion in the sky with the Virgin kneeling, that he had subsequently seen the Virgin many times and that he had seen a vision of what the church building had looked like in the fourteenth century so vivid that he had been able to sketch it, with the result that 'they knew exactly what the porch should look like, and other interesting items'. The boy had seen a 'beautiful lady' who had led him to an area of wall which (investigated without a faculty) had proved to contain two hagioscopes and two aumbries. There had been many other manifestations in the churchyard and rectory grounds, and 'the rector said he believed it to be the wish of Our Lady that the church should be restored to its mediaeval condition, which would cost £800 to £1,000; an appeal was being made for this fund'. FCE was able to recommend to the bishop the name of a member of the Norwich DAC who was a 'good archaeologist and has also specialised in the psychic side of things'. When FCE visited the church, he was unable to obtain access without getting the key, but saw enough to ascertain that the 'hagioscopes and aumbries' were only putlog holes for scaffolding. The villagers too had seen nothing unusual, and in the end they were right. It turned out that the rector had come under the influence of a local man who wanted to create a second Walsingham at Middleton and benefit from the proceeds.

REDUNDANT CHURCHES

The problem of derelict and disused churches (as they were then described) was first discussed by the CCCC in 1922, possibly as a result of a visit made by FCE to Streatley church[29] near Luton, Beds, in July of that year. He asked the Archdeacon of St Albans to bring the matter to the attention of the DAC, writing:

> I never saw anything so dreadful. It is a beautiful church almost entirely mediaeval, yet half the lead is off the south aisle roof, which is full of holes and admitting rain; nearly every window is badly broken, an elder bush is growing in the south aisle, the font steps are covered with moss; the whole place is filthy to the last degree ... It is by far the worst case of neglect that I have ever seen, and I am told that Sundon [held with Streatley], another ancient church, is as bad.

However, 'notwithstanding the neglect the main part of the walls and roof appear sound, and I do not think that any great sum of money will be

FIG 11 A & B *The tower of Streatley, Beds, before and after repair according to SPAB principles under the supervision of F. Lander and Professor Richardson. (Photographs in CCC collection.)*

required to put the whole church into decent order'. He hoped to avoid 'serious public scandal ... I went to Streatley quite accidentally, and if certain journalists happened to do the same they could easily make very serious trouble for the Church'. On 2 August FCE went to Sundon,[30] and found that, although it was a far more important building architecturally, it was in a similar state. It was clear that the building's condition was the result of 'continued neglect, not any great weakness or accidental defect or the result of storms'. In reply, the archdeacon pleaded the legal problems of a parish with no churchwardens or PCC, 'but the Bishop insisted that we could not sit with our hands in our laps and do nothing while two churches fell down – if we can't keep them up we ought to pull them down decently', which was not what FCE had intended. It was not until the 1930s that both churches were restored: Sundon, where the incumbent opposed the granting of the faculty for the restoration, under the direction of W.A. Forsyth; and Streatley, where the tower suffered further damage from use by the Home Guard and could not be tackled until 1948, under the direction of F. Lander; both with guidance from Professor Richardson and financial aid from the Bedfordshire Churches Fund.

Another early case which FCE took up was the village-less church of Winterborne Tomson,[31] Dorset, rebuilt on an ancient site by Archbishop William Wake, in the early eighteenth century, retaining an apsidal east end and some medieval woodwork amongst the Georgian furnishings. The state of the fabric was drawn to FCE's attention in November 1923 by E.T. Long, a convert to Roman Catholicism who was inclined to be critical of the Church of England; he wrote that 'the church is now disused and is apparently to be allowed to go to ruin; can nothing be done?' FCE wrote immediately to the Bishop of Salisbury who referred it to the DAC. Unfortunately the DAC did not live up to expectations: two members knew the church and were reported to 'agree with the Vicar in saying there is nothing of any artistic merit in the church and that, since there is no chance of it being used again, it is generally agreed that the most reverent thing would be to pull it down', a course with which the bishop was inclined to concur. FCE obtained photographs and wrote again to the bishop underlining the architectural importance of the building and diplomatically suggesting that 'in this case I think it would be desirable to come to some arrangement with the Office of Works, which would enable the building to be kept wholly and solely for its historic value, which I gather is greater than has generally been realised'. The upshot was that A.R. Powys, secretary

Fig 12 *Chingford old church in June 1929 after repair by C.C. Winmill. (Photograph by J. Dixon-Scott in CCC collection.)*

of the SPAB, made a report in 1928 and undertook the repair of the church in 1931. When Powys, a member of the famous literary family and a native of Dorchester, died in 1936, he was buried in this churchyard. The church was eventually taken into the care of a national organisation when it was vested in the Redundant Churches Fund in 1974.

A fourth derelict building brought back to use with the encouragement of FCE and restored in accordance with SPAB principles was the old church at Chingford, Essex.[32] After the erection of a church in Chingford Green in 1844–5, the old church had gradually sunk into dereliction, the aisle and nave roofs finally collapsing in February 1904. FCE took the matter up with the Chelmsford DAC in September 1925, and in December 1926 he wrote to the Bishop of Barking:

> the restoration of this church is of much more than local importance. Very hard and unjust things are being said about the church authorities, especially the Church Assembly, at the present time, notably in connexion with the City Churches Bill. Attempts are being made to persuade archaeologists against the Church, and the cry for State Control has been raised in the press. The effect of an announcement, if and when it can be made, will have a re-assuring effect far beyond the locality or the diocese.

A public appeal was launched, and the work was carried out in 1928–30 under the supervision of Charles Canning Winmill (1865–1945).

Perhaps the saddest case was that of the old church at Stoke Mandeville[33], Buckinghamshire. In October 1937 a delegation consisting of Mr C.O. Skilbeck (a member of the CCCC and of the Oxford DAC), W.E. Troke (an architect member of the SPAB), FCE and JDGS visited the ruins in company with the Revd F.J. Winterton, the incumbent. Although the greater parts of the walls of the chancel, nave, south aisle and west tower survived, and were in fair condition, the state of the tower was very bad. A week earlier the problem had reached a crisis when three youths had cycled out from Aylesbury and interfered with loose stonework of the tower, causing several tons of stonework to collapse and kill one of them, a tragic consummation of a series of acts of sacrilege and vandalism. The delegation considered that the building could still be rescued from further decay and reinstated for preservation and use if sufficient money were forthcoming. But the village also had a Victorian church and the vicar had not been prepared to raise funds for the old church since his arrival in 1908; indeed, his solution was to blow up the tower which, the delegation felt, would cause widespread scandal. They noted new houses near the ruined church and thought it quite possible that, as at Chingford, the population of the area might soon increase. But the impasse was never broken, and the recently revised volume of *The Buildings of England: Buckinghamshire* (1994) records laconically that 'The ruins of OLD ST MARY were blown up in 1966'.

The passing of the Union of Benefices Measure in 1924 allowed the erection of a new church and the demolition or appropriation to limited secular uses of an old one not only where benefices had been united but also where 'for any other reason' a church was no longer used or needed. The consent of both Houses of Parliament, the archbishop, the bishop and (if there were burials in the church) the Home Secretary was required. If a church were to be demolished, provision had to be made for the transfer of the font, communion table and plate to another church. There was no mention of consultation with any historic buildings organisation such as the CCCC or SPAB.

In 1938, the year of the Faculty Jurisdiction Measure, the Council expressed concern at the destruction of redundant churches of historic interest in town centres, noting the unfortunate reactions from the Church's critics. The example of the museum created in St Peter Hungate, Norwich, was given to counterbalance the less happy cases of St John Micklegate, York, and several Worcester churches.

It was hoped that statutory provision could be made for all proposals for removing churches to be referred to DACs for advice, though later the Council decided that it should itself be consulted in all cases. In 1941 the Diocesan Reorganisation Committees Measure established committees to recommend to bishops what changes in pastoral supervision would be required as a result of war damage, especially in cities such as Plymouth, including 'the restoration or disposal of churches ... or the site thereof', and allowed the restoration of a damaged church to be deferred for up to five years pending discussions about its future. The committees could co-opt a DAC member if they thought fit; many relied on the overlapping membership of archdeacons. In the same year the CCCC protested to the Government that churches had been put in a third category for war damage claims, after dwellings and commercial buildings.

The Reorganisation Areas Measure 1944 allowed the Ecclesiastical Commissioners to make schemes for the restoration, rebuilding or demolition of war-damaged churches. The CCCC 'or any other body concerned with the care of ancient buildings' was entitled to make representations to the Commissioners upon a scheme being drafted if the scheme 'might affect prejudicially any building of archaeological, historical or artistic interest' and obliged them then to seek the advice of the Royal Fine Art Commission. In the following year the CCCC expressed anxiety about proposals to transfer some derelict churches to America and some to the Ministry of Works, but decided to make no representations until more information had been gathered.

In 1949 the Pastoral Reorganisation Measure was passed, which established Diocesan Pastoral Committees, and in the same year a Church Assembly committee[34] recommended that currently disused churches should be divided into three categories: some 128 'churches and ruins of really outstanding merit' should be handed over to the care of the Ancient Monuments Board of the Ministry of Works, provided that they could be brought back into use in the future if required; some 175 churches, 'a group of very poor buildings, and ruins too fragmentary to retain any interest', should be demolished and their sites sold or left decent; and the 109 remaining churches should have other uses found for them. The report was adopted by Church Assembly, and resulted in the Union of Benefices (Disused Churches) Measure 1952, which provided for the CCCC to be consulted. In its 12th Report (for 1951–6), the Council noted that, although the demolition of four churches of unquestionable historic value was then under consideration, in the 12 years since the war,

> Apart from some 120 19th-century buildings, the demolition of only two late and poor 18th-century churches, two churches containing slight remains of mediaeval work and a barn-like chapel of uncertain date has actually been authorised; this compares very favourably with the number of historic houses which, in spite of legislation, have been demolished in the same period.

Throughout this period it remained possible to demolish churches by faculty. Although chancellors could seek the advice of the DAC if they thought fit, the faculty jurisdiction did not oblige them to consult any national organisation, and this method was therefore considered to be unsatisfactory both by the CCCC and by external critics. (The option of demolishing a church by faculty still remains in parallel with the provisions of the Pastoral Measure, but only in restricted cases involving retention of part of the existing building or rebuilding on the same site.)

In rare cases churches could also be demolished under private Acts of Parliament.

THE SECOND WORLD WAR AND ITS CONSEQUENCES

The 9th Report for 1941–45 records the extent of war damage to English churches: the loss of 'only one mediaeval church of the first rank, Coventry Cathedral', with Great Yarmouth placed in the second rank and two in London (All Hallows Barking and St Olave Hart Street) and two in Bristol (St Peter and Holy Cross (Temple)) and 'perhaps St Martin, Coney Street, York and St Andrew Plymouth' in the third rank. Fourteen other medieval churches were mentioned as almost completely destroyed, including five in Norwich, but none of the best medieval roofs had been lost apart from Coventry, no major wooden screens, and very little ancient glass thanks to their removal in time. The losses of 'Renaissance' churches were far greater because so many of the best examples stood in towns. Sixteen Wren churches in the City had been very severely damaged (of which nine have since been rebuilt and one transported to America), as well as St Clement Danes, St Anne Soho, and St James Piccadilly, together with Hawksmoor's St George in the East and the parish church of Islington. Because the Temple Church was reckoned to be

> practically a facsimile, so completely were its surfaces renewed a century ago, another similar process, now inevitable, will bring no loss, but there has been an irreparable loss here in the destruction of the splendid series

of Renaissance monuments hidden away in the clearstorey of the round church.

The list continues with examples from the 'Waterloo period' and, from the Victorian, Pearson's St John, Red Lion Square, Holborn, and G.G. Scott Junior's St Agnes, Kennington. 'Some students of Victorian architecture would also include Butterfield's churches of St Alban Holborn and St Clement City Road.' Other Victorian losses were passed over quickly in order to concentrate on the loss of furnishings, especially from the City churches. Details were also given of the damage to cathedrals.

On the other hand, the war had, perhaps surprisingly, encouraged an upsurge in artistic endeavour in churches, which was fostered by a travelling exhibition, 'The Artist and the Church' assembled by John Piper for the Council for the Encouragement of Music and the Arts (later to become the Arts Council). The CCCC was gratified, noting that the Church should not allow cultural values to be eclipsed by the war. The Report drew special attention to Henry Moore's *Madonna and Child* in St Matthew, Northampton, Hans Feibusch's mural paintings at St Elisabeth, Eastbourne, and Eric Kennington's recumbent effigy of Lawrence of Arabia at St Martin, Wareham, in addition to a number of stained glass windows. A remarkable architectural achievement was Professor Richardson's timber church at All Hallows, Greenford, 'a highly original and striking building', built under special licence from the Government using imported timber from Canada.

That Report reminded the public that the Central Council and the Diocesan Committees had 'neither the powers nor the money, nor the labour to carry out salvage work'. The next Report (the 10th) published in 1947, responded to press criticism that the Church had neglected to protect her treasures from the risk of damage during the war years by setting out details of what FCE and JDGS had achieved. FCE had taken advantage of his position as a Governor of St Audries' School, in West Somerset, to persuade the Misses Townshend, the owner–headmistresses, to allow use of the large stone-built cellars as stores for furniture from the London City churches. Eventually 29 lorry-loads including six reredoses, two chancel screens, fifteen pulpits, three churchwardens' pews, doorcases from three churches, and two organs were deposited there. The crypt of Wiveliscombe church, rebuilt in 1826, was unusually large and dry, and could be used for fragile objects such as the Gospel Book of St Chad from Lichfield. A third location found by FCE was the cellar of a farmhouse high up on Exmoor, where valuable plate was deposited.

Items removed to store included the early Saxon cross from Leeds Parish Church; the Scottish lectern looted from Holyrood (then in St Stephen, St Albans, and since stolen, probably by Scottish nationalists); the medieval painted panels from St Michael at Plea, housed in a chapel of Norwich Cathedral; and the 'little known' retable from Thornham Parva, Suffolk. Such diverse objects as early bells from London churches, the stalls from Lancaster Priory, the brasses from St Mary Redcliffe, valuable communion plate and church records from St Dunstan in the West (London), New Romney (Kent), St Pancras (London), Horsey (Norfolk), Yardley (Birmingham), Lancaster Priory, and many other places, were all safeguarded, either in the church, in a secure place nearby or under the charge of the CCCC in Somerset. Such care was also extended to objects from outside the Church of England, such as seven chandeliers and ten candlesticks from Bevis Marks Synagogue in the City of London; chandeliers, liturgical ornaments, portraits and other objects from the United Synagogue; 19 cases of records from Guildhall Library; 25 crates containing the Huguenot library from the French Protestant Church in Soho Square, London; charters and books from Sherborne School Library; and a triptych and glass from the Sherborne Almshouse chapel.

The Report went on to point out that

among the artistic treasures of this country there is nothing more valuable or more beautiful than the comparatively scanty remains of ancient glass, and certainly nothing more fragile. When it is realised that the greater part of it was removed to safety or otherwise protected all through the war, some idea can be obtained of the magnitude of the work involved. The cost has been enormous. The opportunity has been and is being taken to execute repairs and re-leading, so that in most cases the glass will eventually be in better condition than it has been for very many years.

Amazingly, little medieval glass was destroyed: in London the only remaining figure from the glass of Henry VII's Chapel in Westminster Abbey and a little in the provincial churches of Dibden (Hants), Clyst St George (Devon), and St Martin Coney Street, York. An early sixteenth-century window at Basingstoke, the seventeenth-century east window of Shoreditch and the eighteenth-century east window of St Andrew Holborn were serious losses from later periods. Glass removed to safety included many windows at Canterbury and Exeter (fortunately, for the cathedral was badly bombed) Cathedrals; the great east window at St Peter Mancroft,

Norwich; and the windows at Fairford (Glos), Malvern Priory, Selby Abbey, Beverley Minster, the Burne Jones windows at Allerton (Lancs); Thornhill and Elland (Yorks); Selling (Kent); Kingsland (Herefs); Hingham, East Harling and North Tuddenham (Norfolk); King's College Chapel, Cambridge; St George's Chapel, Windsor; Bere Ferrers (Devon); All Saints North Street, St Denys Walmgate, St Michael le Belfry, Holy Trinity Goodramgate, St Martin Coney Street and St Michael Spurriergate, all in York; Wilton (Wilts); Walton in Gordano (Somerset); Nettlestead (Kent). Post-Reformation glass was not ignored, such as the heraldic glass at Battersea, the west window of St Andrew Undershaft, City of London (subsequently severely damaged by the St Mary Axe bomb in 1992), and 'a great deal of modern [i.e. Victorian and later] glass'.

Although the CCCC had no statutory involvement with the rebuilding of war-damaged churches, it did take great interest in specific cases. One was St Agnes, Kennington Park,[35] designed by George Gilbert Scott Junior and now generally recognised to have been an outstanding building. The CCCC architect member, S.E. Dykes Bower, reported to the vicar in August 1946 that although the roof of the nave and chancel and most of the stone tracery of the east window had gone in the bombing, 'the main fabric of the church remains and is substantially sound'; restoration would cost the equivalent of 75 per cent of a new church. 'St Agnes was not merely one of the most beautiful churches in London; it is one of the really notable works of its time and as such deserves full restoration.' FCE wrote to Dykes Bower, 'I do know about the difficulties there: the trouble is that the church is really not wanted as it is so close to two others.' Nevertheless he felt that 'the church is architecturally of such importance that it is rather more than a merely diocesan question', and he decided to fight for it, writing to the Bishop of Kingston (who was also the archdeacon) that

> St Agnes is, or was, one of the finest of the Gothic Revival churches, and one of very few by the younger Scott, who left us very little, and its destruction would do a lot of harm to the good name of the Church which would far outweigh any small immediate advantage.

He even went so far as to suggest that the Greek Revival church of St Mark, which had lost its roof, might be demolished instead, but was told that St Mark's was one of the liveliest parishes in the archdeaconry. The PCC of St Agnes wanted a smaller church for easy heating. FCE was not moved, replying that

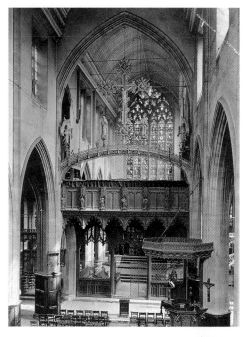

FIG 13 A & B St Agnes, Kennington before and after war damage, showing the complete shell remaining in sound condition. (Latter photograph by Gordon Barnes in CCC collection.)

the great Perpendicular churches of East Anglia, the Fens and Yorkshire are *and always have been* far in excess of the practical needs of the population ... and just as no-one dreams of pulling down one of those great churches because it is over-large, so no-one should on purely utilitarian grounds condemn this great church.

By July 1953 Dykes Bower had resigned as the parish architect, but the CCC fought on, using every available ally – Ivor Bulmer-Thomas and the newly formed Historic Churches Preservation Trust, the War Damage Commission, John Betjeman and Walter Godfrey. In the end, however, the battle was lost and the ruins were taken down. The surviving furnishings and glass were mostly re-used by Dykes Bower at Holy Spirit Southsea, a large church by J.T. Micklethwaite which he was rebuilding after war damage. The vicar of St Agnes did, however, confess to a doubt: 'We hope Mr Covell's church will not look too small beside the big flats which the LCC proposes to build.'

During the war the care of churches was neglected, due both to the absence of many people on active service and to the use sometimes made of parts of churches, especially towers, by the regular forces and the Home Guard. As a result the CCCC offered practical advice in two leaflets, *How to Protect A Church in Wartime* (1940), and *Church Towers and Bells in Wartime* (1942). After the war the CCCC persuaded the Chancellor of the Exchequer to rescind Purchase Tax on church textiles and to extend the exemption of war memorials from Purchase Tax until 1955. Concessions were negotiated with the Ministry of Fuel and Power on petrol for DAC members, and with the Board of Trade on gold leaf for church use, subject to FCE's approval.

Before the war FCE had been sole co-ordinator of DACs, monitoring their work by constantly travelling to attend their meetings and visit churches with them, all the time encouraging them to maintain uniform standards. During and after the war, when restrictions made it impossible to travel on this scale, another way had to be found to encourage DACs to adopt a common approach, for example, in encouraging better designs for war memorials. Thus the first residential conference was held for DAC Chairmen and Secretaries of the Southern Province at Farnham Castle in September 1946, when 23 of the 27 dioceses were represented; it was followed by one for the Northern Province at St William's College, York, in June 1947. A further conference was held at Wadham College, Oxford, in April 1953, and later these conferences became annual and open to all

DAC members and members of kindred organisations. The first conference for cathedral architects was held in May 1948 and the second in 1952, since when conferences have been held triennially.

The war also concentrated the CCCC's mind on the establishment of a national survey of churches, an aspect of work which, though it had been mentioned in the early days as fundamental, had only grown haphazardly because of other pressures. In 1935 the Courtauld Institute had offered to act as the central repository for photographs, plans and other information, but the CCCC felt that the Church ought to provide this itself. When, early in 1941, the National Buildings Record[36] was established to record all buildings of historic and architectural interest threatened by damage or loss in the war, the CCCC Chairman and Professor Richardson were appointed members of its Advisory Council (upon which such representation continued until the absorption in 1963 of the National Buildings Record (NBR) into the Royal Commission on the Historical Monuments of England). In its turn, the CCCC stimulated the interest of amateur photographers and obtained petrol allowances for them, with the intention that copies of the resulting prints should eventually be available in Church

FIG 14 *The first conference of cathedral architects, held at Lincoln in 1948, showing (from left) Leslie Moore (Peterborough), H.M. Drury (Exeter), A.B. Whittingham (Norwich), FCE, JDGS, Canon A.G. Cooke (Sub-Dean), W.A. Forsyth (Blackburn, Rochester and Salisbury), unidentified, B. Parsons (Salisbury), Ian Lindsay (Newcastle), Robert Godfrey (Lincoln). (Photograph by* Lincolnshire Echo.)

House, the diocese and the parish. The scheme was publicised by the BBC and the press, and FCE estimated that over 700 people became involved, co-ordinated by the CCCC. By the end of 1942 the CCCC held about 50,000 photographs, and by the end of 1944 (when the NBR held about 200,000) this figure had almost trebled to 130,000, rising by the end of 1946 to about 150,000, many of which were duplicated to the NBR. Some are evocative of the period, such as the extensive coverage of West Midlands churches, and in particular their fonts, taken by Miss Heather Sanderson Stewart who attached typewritten notes with her reactions to the buildings, the problems of access, the attitude of the incumbent, the state of the churchyard and the difficulties of getting petrol. In 1949, when the survey was valued at £24,000, FCE estimated that during the five years of its greatest growth, 1943–8, it had only cost £934. The results of this astonishing effort helped greatly with the accurate restoration of damaged churches after the war, and still form the basis of the Council's nationwide survey of parish churches.

After the war the Council decided that ordination candidates should receive at their theological colleges some preliminary training in the care of churches, for which all of them would in due course become responsible. The first series of lantern slides with duplicated notes was prepared by W.I. Croome in 1949, when he reported that every college had accepted either one or three of the lectures. In November 1963 it was reported that 20 colleges had regular, if infrequent, lectures on the care of churches, but within two years they had mostly lapsed and it has proved impossible to resuscitate them on a regular basis.

CATHEDRALS

Although the advisory system was originally designed for parish churches which fell within the faculty jurisdiction, and could not apply to cathedrals, it was not forgotten that it had been the cathedrals which under the bill of 1913 would have been brought within state control. Deans, provosts and chapters remained jealous of their independence, but referred some cases to the CCCC. In 1931, for example, it expressed anxiety about W.D. Caröe's proposals to remove the spires added by his master, Ewan Christian, to the west towers of Southwell Minster. In 1933, at the request of the Dean and Chapter of Salisbury, who were anxious about low-flying aircraft circling the spire during aviation displays, the CCCC persuaded the Air Ministry to issue a notice to airmen, *Low Flying over Cathedrals, Churches and Old and*

Historic Buildings. Some other cases referred to the CCCC included the proposed extension of Portsmouth Cathedral by Sir Charles Nicholson (1933), the new pulpit by Leslie Moore at Peterborough (1935), and the conservative treatment of the mutilated Lady Chapel reredos at Ely by placing a free-standing altar and riddel-posts in front of it (1938); all of which were approved. On the other hand, the Council expressed strong opposition to the proposed removal of Scott's chancel screen at Hereford in 1934 and again in 1939 (it was removed in 1966). After the war, the Council welcomed the decision to replace Bodley's reredos at St Paul's by a baldacchino designed by S.E. Dykes Bower and W. Godfrey Allen (1948). The Council also warmly supported a proposal to add a rood loft, rood and decorated tympanum designed by Comper to the Jacobean screen at Wakefield (1950).

The CCCC's involvement with the rebuilding of Coventry Cathedral showed the shortcomings of the informal arrangements. The Provost had written as early as 1941 to say that it had been decided to rebuild the cathedral on the same site and that this could be done in one of three ways – as a facsimile of the old building; by erecting a new building 'in some modern style'; or by erecting a new building generally in sympathy with, but not a copy of, the old. The CCCC favoured the last option and advised the Provost not to hold a competition but to approach four architects: W.H. Randoll Blacking, S.E. Dykes Bower, Leslie Moore and Sir Albert Richardson. The Provost replied that he wished to approach Giles Scott, and six months later wrote to say that the chapter had appointed him. The CCCC said that he had not been on its list because it had only recommended architects not already working on new cathedrals (Scott was in the middle of the construction of Liverpool Cathedral). Ten years later the situation had changed again – Basil Spence was now the architect, and a special meeting of CCCC was called on 3 April 1952 for him to present his designs. 'Those present', the minutes record, 'were impressed by Mr Spence's thoughtfulness and originality in facing the problems of the difficult circumstances at Coventry', and they were reassured about the state of the old tower and spire. After he had left the room, the Council agreed that it was 'unsatisfactory that the cathedral should be arranged as if it was merely a large parish church' because this would perpetuate a Victorian mistake.

Meanwhile, in 1949, Lord Methuen, anxious about unspecified 'recent activities' at Gloucester and Norwich, had advocated the formation of a

Cathedrals Committee, and was told that this was already being discussed with deans and provosts. They agreed that the committee was a good idea, but they could not bind themselves to consult it. The Cathedrals Advisory Committee came into being early in 1950 under the chairmanship of Dean Cranage. Although its status was increasingly strengthened on several occasions, for too many years deans and provosts consulted it only as they wished.

NEW CHURCHES

Another category of building which did not come within the remit of the CCCC or the DACs was that of new churches, since until they have been consecrated they remain outside the faculty jurisdiction. This caused (and still causes) the anomalous situation that, while the DAC has not been allowed any part in the design or fitting out of a new church, immediately upon consecration of the building it becomes responsible for advising the chancellor about any changes to it. Comper took advantage of this by delaying the consecration of St Mary Wellingborough until it had been built and furnished entirely to his satisfaction, so that the Peterborough DAC should have no say in any aspect of it.

The problem was later to be described as

the Church of England's failure to seize an opportunity such as is unlikely to recur, all the more tragic in view of what has been happening during the same period in other countries; ... whereas on the Continent church architecture has been in deep communication with theology and liturgy since the early 20s, in this country it has been carried on in an aesthetic vacuum and treated as something quite peripheral to the Church's pastoral and missionary task; the preserve of antiquarians, archdeacons, secretaries of boards of finance and church-furnishers. [37]

The matter was first aired in the CCCC in 1931, and in the following year a letter was sent to all bishops asking them to seek the informal advice of their DACs. This was not motivated by a dislike of particular new churches. FCE praised several modern designs, in particular Welch Cachemaille-Day and Lander's St Saviour, Eltham, which was illustrated in the Report for 1932–3, the same architects' St Nicholas, Burnage (Manchester), and suburban London churches by Giles Scott, Martin Travers, Edward Maufe and Charles Nicholson. Not much seems to have resulted, for a similar letter had to be sent to bishops in 1953, when attention was also drawn to the embarrassment caused by bishops dedicating new furnishings which had been installed in churches without faculty. The example of the Bishop of Gloucester, who had decided to ask the churchwardens to produce the faculty as part of the dedication ceremony, was commended.

NEW WORKS OF ART

The post-war years saw the introduction of the first wave of modernist works of art into churches. At first the Council was wary of recommending them. Some members hoped that what they liked to call 'amateur art', because it fell outside the usual bounds of ecclesiastical craftsmanship,

FIG 15 The Virgin and Child *by Henry Moore, 1943 and 1949, for the church at Claydon, Suffolk.*

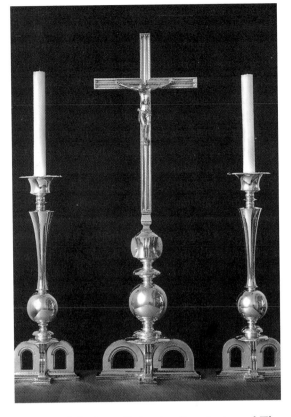

Fig 16 *Cross and candlesticks for the memorial chapel of the King's Shropshire Light Infantry and the Herefordshire Regiment in St Chad, Shrewsbury, designed by Bernard Miller and made by W. Knight of Wellingborough; the photograph was used in a CCCC exhibition in the early 1950s as an example of good modern work. (Photograph in CCC collection.)*

would be a passing phase. Its view of Graham Sutherland's painting of *The Crucifixion* in St Matthew, Northampton in 1947 was, however, that 'while works of art of this kind may not appeal to a number of people, it is right that the Church should be ready to explore new artistic works of every kind'. When in 1948 it was proposed to install a statue of *The Virgin and Child* by Henry Moore as a war memorial in the church at Claydon, Suffolk, some members of the Council formed a strong dislike for sculptures of this school. It was finally agreed that 'the introduction of work by so eminent a sculptor into such a church [that is, one largely rebuilt to designs probably prepared by the incumbent in 1862] should not be opposed'. This decision was influenced by the redoutable figure of Sir Eric Maclagan, Director of the V&A, who said that he would resign from the CCCC if it was opposed.

In the catalogue of the exhibition *Art in the Service of the Church*, held in Lambeth Palace as the Church of England's contribution to the Festival of

Britain in 1951, FCE noted in a brief historical survey entitled 'The Artist's Debt to the Past', that

> ultimately the artist must acknowledge at heart how much he owes to tradition, but he is also influenced by those strange waves of taste with their inevitable reactions, which in their more extreme forms become a great danger ... at the moment we are witnessing the growth of a new outlook which seeks to preserve and protect all good and characteristic work whatever its nature.

It was an outlook which he himself had done much to foster.

Part 2
Expansion and consolidation
1954–96

4
Expansion

PROGRESS IN THE CARE OF BUILDINGS

The mid-1950s were a time of great change for the Council. They brought within the space of two or three years a new constitution, and changes of chairman and secretary, of office location and of general outlook. In the Church of England at large there was a growing desire to be freed from the rigorous liturgical rules promoted between 1900 and 1939, which was expressed in increasing interest in other liturgies which were now recognised as contributing something towards Anglican forms of worship instead of being seen as dangerous deviations from them. In 1948 Addleshaw and Etchells[1] proposed that the arrangement of churches for modern use might be based on mid-seventeenth-century Laudian precedent rather than the use of 1548–9; in 1960 Peter Hammond,[2] greatly influenced by the Parish and People movement, urged the study of contemporary Continental and American churches and their liturgical arrangements.

In the wider world of what was beginning to be called conservation, there were developments in secular legislation. In 1932 the first Town and Country Planning Act, promoted by Sir Hilton Young (later first Lord Kennet), created building perservation orders, and in 1944 a revised Act introduced the concept of listing buildings of architectural and historic importance in order to protect them, a provision supplemented by the necessary finance in the Historic Buildings and Ancient Monuments Act of 1953 which established the Historic Buildings Council and provided funds for it to allocate in grant aid towards the restoration of secular buildings. The Local Authorities (Historic Buildings) Act 1962 made more funds available and gave local authorities the discretion to offer grants for historic buildings including churches. Later revisions of the Town and Country Planning Act introduced further refinements such as spot listing, conservation areas, and tree preservation orders. After the war the Land Fund was created and given £50 million to spend in purchase of threatened landscapes in memory of those who had died in the wars, but the money was gradually diverted to other purposes. The initiative was revitalised by the creation of the National Heritage Memorial Fund in 1980, provided with an initial grant of nearly £12.5 million. This has recently been supplemented by the far larger funds made available from the National Lottery during 1995.

The campaigning SPAB had been augmented by an offshoot, the Georgian Group, in 1937. In 1958 they were joined by the Victorian Society. More recently still, in the 1980s, the Thirties Society has brought the amenity societies up to the present by re-naming itself the Twentieth Century Society.

The benefits of the ecclesiastical exemption have remained under review throughout the Council's history, and from time to time come into prominence, usually in the wake of a *cause célèbre*. One such moment was the result of a strange decision by the Court of Appeal in 1964 that a parsonage house, the rectory of St George Bloomsbury (6, Gower Street, London WC1), was 'a building in ecclesiastical use', which, as the amenity societies immediately pointed out in a letter to *The Times*, meant that a whole category of listed buildings ceased to be subject to listed buildings controls as well as falling outside the faculty jurisdiction. While this matter remained unresolved, the vicarage designed by J.D. Sedding, linked to his church of St Clement, Bournemouth, by a passageway, was demolished. A later review, undertaken by the Faculty Jurisdiction Commission in 1980–4, led to the legislation currently in force.

LOCATION OF OFFICES

The change of location came about in summer 1955. For some time after the end of the war, Church House remained requisitioned by the Government, and the size of the Council's library and photographic archive made rental of suitable premises elsewhere in central London prohibitive. So the Council remained at Dunster for ten years after the end of the war until, with FCE's death, his house was no longer available. Returning to London, the CCCC took five rooms in the Tudor Courtyard of Fulham Palace, then still the residence of the Bishop of London, as tenants of the Church Commissioners. This was only a short-term solution. Within four years a new idea arose out of anxiety about those London City churches which remained unrestored after war damage. In a letter to *The Times* in June 1958 the Council expressed concern that the diocese was having difficulty in meeting the cost of the restoration of the last few churches. The Council hoped that St Katherine Cree, SS Anne and Agnes, St Andrew by the Wardrobe, St Nicholas Cole Abbey and All Hallows London Wall might be restored, that the towers of Christ Church Newgate Street, St Dunstan in the East and St Michael Paternoster Royal might be retained, and that St Mary Aldermanbury might be retained if possible. Later in the year the Archdeacon of London reported that, although a quarter of the damaged City churches had yet to be restored, and despite inflation, he hoped that both St Andrew by the Wardrobe and St Nicholas Cole Abbey might be rebuilt. The Diocesan Reorganisation Committee eventually managed to provide for the restoration of all these churches with the exception of Christ Church, where the tower only remains, and St Dunstan, where the roofless shell formed an enclosed garden.

In November 1958, the idea was floated that the CCCC might help to solve the problem of one of the City churches by offering to use All Hallows London Wall[3] as its headquarters after restoration. It is a simple yet elegant mid-eighteenth-century church, designed by George Dance the younger immediately after his return from Italy. In its light airiness it contrasts markedly with the churches of Wren but, perhaps for this reason, its qualities had not been widely appreciated. In addition to providing office space, the church could be used as a Christian Arts Centre, offering exhibitions and lectures as well as services for City workers and others. The

FIG 17 *Robert Stopford, Bishop of London, rededicating All Hallows, London Wall, on 10 July 1962; he is flanked by Dean Seiriol Evans on his left and the Revd E.C.E. Bourne on his right. (Photograph by Central Press Photos Ltd.)*

proposal was welcomed by the bishop and the diocese, and in February 1959 approved by the Guild Church Council of All Hallows. In the next month David Nye was appointed architect, the approval of the Central Board of Finance obtained and CCCC nominees were added to the church's Electoral Roll. Towards the end of that year the Council approved Nye's plans for restoration and refurnishing. Early in 1960 they were recommended by the London DAC, and the faculty was granted. The builders were Dove Brothers and the cost, about £47,000, was met by the diocese with help from the War Damage Commission. The extra cost of about £8,200 for the restoration of the church rooms to an enlarged design to form offices was paid for by the CBF on behalf of the CCCC. The Council first met at All Hallows on 17 May 1962, shortly before the restoration was completed. On 10 July 1962 the church was rededicated by the Bishop of London at a Solemn Eucharist in the morning, followed in the afternoon by a service of thanksgiving and dedication with a sermon by Archbishop Michael Ramsey.

At this time the word 'Central' was dropped from the title of the Council. It has since remained 'The Council for the Care of Churches', with the exception of a period from January 1972 until spring 1981 when it was known as 'The Council for Places of Worship'.

The Buckley Commission on the City Churches, which reported in 1972, recommended that the Council should remain at All Hallows. The intention was that the church should be declared redundant, but this has not come about, even though suggested on several subsequent occasions. After exhibitions ceased to be held in 1970, it was possible to move the library and the council meeting room, both hitherto located in cramped conditions, into the body of the church. David Nye had retired as architect and so the Council commissioned a scheme from Raymond Erith, an architect responsible for much work in a sympathetic Georgian style. His handsome proposal proved too elaborate and costly and, when he died early in 1974, the Council decided that instead of attempting to furnish the building in keeping with the style of the architecture, it would be more practical to install functional wooden bookcases stained to match the existing Georgian woodwork. Fine new meeting tables were made by Nicholas Partridge and Norman Illingworth in 1987.

Early in 1993 George Carey, Archbishop of Canterbury, was warmly welcomed on a visit to All Hallows, when he worshipped with the staff, and heard short presentations on the Council's work. Soon after, however, that

FIG 18 *George Carey, Archbishop of Canterbury, with Christopher Campling (Dean of Ripon), Chairman of the CCC, Mrs Hester Agate, OBE, Vice-Chairman, Miss Judith Scott, OBE, Mr Timothy Robinson (Secretary, Central Board of Finance), Mr Edward Peacock (Administrative Secretary to the Archbishop), and members of staff of the Council for the Care of Churches and Cathedrals Fabric Commission for England, 1993. (Photograph by Malcolm Crowthers.)*

work was severely disrupted by the terrorist bomb explosion in Bishopsgate on 24 April 1993, which blew in every window in the building, caused structural damage to the roof, walls and decorative plasterwork and damaged office furniture. The church remained scaffolded for most of the year while repairs were carried out under the supervision of Caroe and Partners, co-ordinated by Jonathan Goodchild in his capacity as Guild Church Clerk. Meetings of the Council and its committees had to be held elsewhere. The opportunity was taken to redecorate the church interior to an eighteenth-century colour scheme devised by Dr Ian Bristow. The work of returning the church interior as nearly as possible to its eighteenth-century appearance has continued with the inscription of the Ten Commandments, Belief and Lord's Prayer by Kevin Glashier in the panels of the apse and the creation of a new chandelier by Antiquities Ltd to match the single survivor of the original pair made by Lukyn Betts in 1765.

The Council remained at All Hallows until changing circumstances meant that the church had become an increasingly cramped and unsuitable home for the organisation, and in December 1994 the headquarters was moved for the fifth time, to Fielden House, Little College Street, Westminster, the nearest the Council has yet come to fulfilling the pre-war prospect of offices within Church House.

CHAIRMEN, SECRETARIES AND MEMBERS

The retirement of Dean Cranage in 1953 caused a flurry of letters between the office and Eric Milner-White, Dean of York and Vice-Chairman of the CCCC, about a successor. Milner-White wrote to FCE on 27 March 1953

Perhaps I can guess what Cranage's message is? If it be that he is resigning, you will want a new Chairman. Let me at once, as Vice-Chairman, say how willing I would be to serve in the higher office, even delighted – but I have now, alas, ceased to be my own master. Two things quite put any nomination of myself out of practical politics.

They were the distance from York and the fact that his recent illness had been attributed to over-work. But there was an obvious candidate:

My own suggestion for the Chairmanship would be Seiriol [S.J.A. Evans, Archdeacon of Wisbech and Secretary of the Ely DAC for some years, recently appointed Dean of Gloucester]. He is not a specially popular speaker in C.A., but is adequate. The rise in his dignity is all-important and we may be certain that he will rise to it and gain in weight. He really *does* know the business and is a kindly chairman; and as one of my own dear sons in God, knows me well enough to talk anything over, should he wish, at any moment.

The succession to the secretaryship in the following year, after FCE's death in August 1954, was less sure. Perhaps the new chairman had not quite found his feet; there was certainly anxiety in the minds of some clergy members of the Council that, in a world dominated by men, a woman would be unable to hold her own as secretary. Whatever the reason, the obvious candidate, trained by FCE and a devoted servant of CCCC for the past 18 years, was not appointed. Instead, the Council decided that it would be better to have someone with the right paper qualifications, and appointed Francis Ian Gregory Rawlins, Deputy Keeper and Chief Scientific Adviser to the National Gallery and Secretary General of the International Institute for Conservation of Museum Objects, as part-time Secretary. Rawlins was a devout Anglo-Catholic bachelor, a quiet man of delicate health and 'an exquisite and sensitive courtesy',[4] temperamentally ill-suited to piloting an expanding organisation through sometimes troubled waters. Because he found it difficult to reconcile the divisive demands made on him by the

National Gallery and the CCCC, his health suffered, and in summer 1956 his doctor advised him to decide between the two; he chose the former, continuing with CCCC in the non-administrative role of Technical Director until his sudden death in May 1969.

Then another obstacle presented itself: the Secretary of the Central Board of Finance asked that appointments of secretaries to Church Assembly boards should be deferred for the time being, pending re-organisation. John Betjeman, amongst others, was outraged and wrote to JDGS on 20 October 1956 with characteristic vigour:

> I am horrified at the position you are in and I am thinking of resigning from the Central Council unless you can persuade me it is worth belonging. It looks to me as though it has become a conspiracy of archdeacons ... I can understand that old Ivor Thomas may be difficult to work with, but I do not feel at all safe with these smooth administrative clerics with no aesthetic feeling, only organisational ability. The Church Assembly is the place for them, not the Central Council. Please advise me. I will telephone to you to save you the trouble of writing.
>
> Archdeacons make me lose my faith. Love and Kisses, John Betjeman.

JDGS was eventually appointed secretary on 30 June in the following year.

Dean Evans, Will Croome and JDGS formed a strong team, in spite of the occasional friction between Chairman and Vice-Chairman to be expected from such strong characters, until Will Croome's death in 1967. When Dean Evans became Chairman, FCE had made no bones about the problem, writing on 1 April 1953,

> The position in the last few years has been quite fantastic; our chairman has always been most kind and ready in signing letters which we have sent to him, sometimes quite a number of them. But the advice on every matter of policy has been obtained elsewhere, for the most part from Croome who has a good clear head and is readily available on the telephone.

Dean Evans amply fulfilled FCE's hopes, and Will Croome continued to help, not only on matters of policy but with a host of other things through trenchantly expressed letters which passed between Gloucestershire and London.

Born in 1894, educated at King's School, Worcester and King's College, Cambridge, Seiriol Evans had been Precentor and Headmaster of the Choir School at Ely from 1923 to 1929, Rector of Upwell from 1929 to 1939, a naval chaplain in the war, and Archdeacon of Wisbech from 1945 until

1953 when he was appointed to the Deanery of Gloucester; he had also been Secretary of the Ely DAC from 1930 to 1953. He was said by the *Church Times* to be the best-dressed clergyman of his generation, and he certainly had a decanal presence, tempered with a kindly disposition. His breadth of interest in historical matters was recognised by his membership of the Royal Commission on Historical Manuscripts from 1957 and his appointment as a Trustee of the National Portrait Gallery in 1963. After he retired from 17 years' service as Chairman of the Council at the end of 1971, he remained chairman of the Conservation Committee until 1981. Having moved from Gloucester back to Cambridgeshire, he was appointed Chairman of the Ely DAC, a post which he held almost until his death in 1984 aged 90.

William Iveson Croome was an even more remarkable man. Born in 1891 he had been educated at Malvern College and New College, Oxford. His youthful enthusiasm for church art and architecture had been kindled by the architects F.C. Eden and Walter Tapper, who often took him on their annual tours on the Continent. His retentive and accurate memory for what he saw was only equalled by that of FCE himself. Although his poor eyesight had prevented him from serving in the First World War, his experience as a hospital administrator trying to cope with the needs of wounded and dying soldiers brought back from the trenches in France aroused in him a concern for human suffering which complemented his perception of church architecture and liturgy as lively instruments in the proclamation of the gospel. He remained a bachelor, with private means adequate to allow him to spend all his time working for the good of the Church and the community. His beautifully furnished house, surrounded by a garden in which he took much pleasure, was kept by a cook–housekeeper, and his faithful chauffeur Cyril Mills drove him everywhere. His insomniac disposition allowed him to spend much of the night at his typewriter.

At FCE's instigation, Croome was appointed the first secretary of the Bath and Wells DAC (1919–24). After moving to Gloucestershire he became a member of the Gloucester DAC in 1924, serving as its Secretary from 1926, and Chairman from 1947. At national level he was Chairman of the Grants Committee of the Historic Churches Preservation Trust and a member of the CCCC from 1927, Vice-Chairman of the Standing Committee from 1951 and Chairman of the Wallpaintings Committee (1953–67), Vice-Chairman of the Council and Chairman of the Cathedrals Advisory Committee (both 1955–67). His ideal church was North Cerney,

FIG 19 *North Cerney before the improvements made by Will Croome between 1912 and 1966 (compare Frontispiece). (Photograph in CCC collection.)*

where he was churchwarden and served at the altar each Sunday. It is filled with beautiful objects either given or inspired by him, the first presented on his 21st birthday in 1912.

He contributed to the well-being of Gloucestershire by serving on innumerable committees. He was a County Councillor, a magistrate for 40 years (23 of them as Chairman of the Cirencester bench), 20 years Chairman of the Cotswold Approved School and of the County Probation Committee, and Chairman of the Governors of Barnwood Hospital. On his death Dean Evans recorded that,

> Will Croome belonged to that now almost extinct line of country gentlemen who, being scholars in their own right, placed all their knowledge, expertise and energy at the service of their Church and of their country, for no remuneration at all. But he was not just an amateur; he was a virtuoso.

The truth of this shines out of all the lively letters and reports which repose in the Council's files.

The membership of the Council and its committees since the war has included many notable names: in the museum world, Sir Trenchard Cox, Sir Frank Francis, Edward Croft-Murray and Charles Oman; amongst architects S.E. Dykes Bower, Francis Johnson, Laurence King, Donald Buttress and Alan Rome; amongst antiquarians Joan Evans, Rupert Gunnis, Peter Lasko, Sir Oliver Millar, Pamela Tudor-Craig (Lady Wedgwood); amongst the clergy, Basil Clarke (author of the seminal books *Church Builders of the Nineteenth Century* which appeared as early as 1938 and *The Building of the Eighteenth-Century Church*, both well in advance of their time), Canon C.B. Mortlock, Antony Bridge (Dean of Guildford); and artists such as L.C. Evetts. Academic and televisual prowess were combined in Nancy Wilkinson, Vice-Chairman in the 1980s, who had been the first winner of *Mastermind*. For a time in the early 1950s Ivor Bulmer-Thomas was a member, and the minutes for the period, and that period only, are suddenly full of resolutions proposed and votes taken. His enthusiasms were well-founded, if sometimes intransigently propounded, and it is to his far-sighted tenacity that we owe the Inspection of Churches Measure, the Historic Churches Preservation Trust, the Friends of Friendless Churches, the

FIG 20 *'Deanery Chapter Meeting', a sketch done by Basil Clarke during the CCC Executive Committee meeting on 14 March 1974, typical of many others which were usually hastily destroyed at the end of each meeting. (Private collection.)*

revitalised Ancient Monuments Society and the Churches Conservation Trust.

Three other names deserve special mention. Eric Milner Milner-White[5] (1884–1963) was a member of the Council from 1947, and later its Vice-Chairman and Chairman of the Standing Committee. Described as a shy, reserved man, somewhat precious in speech, he had a wide-ranging knowledge of ecclesiastical arts and crafts, especially stained glass, and architecture. He placed the daily round of worship in the Minster before the fabric and the community, yet he did much for the building, writing in the *Report to the Friends of York Minster* in 1942, shortly after his arrival, 'we shall be united in the passion to make the Minster still more glorious within'. He introduced some furnishings made in Yorkshire by Thompson of Kilburn and others designed by Comper and Richardson, and above all he saw through a campaign of re-instatement, re-arrangement and restoration of the Minster glass after the war. For the Council he wrote a pamphlet *How to Choose Stained Glass* which remained in print for many years. He was Chairman of the York DAC from 1944 until his death, proving to be a strong chairman with decided views, and his enthusiasm for the work of G.G. Pace did much to further the latter's career, though there is nothing by him in the Minster.

Sir Albert Richardson[6] (1880–1964) was an ebullient, merry figure of entirely eighteenth-century character, often dressing in Georgian clothes to suit his beautiful house at Ampthill, Bedfordshire. He was a member of CCCC for 30 years and of the DACs of London, St Albans, Ely and Southwark. He published a number of books on eighteenth-century architecture which advanced public appreciation of the subject, and supervised the post-war restorations of St James, Piccadilly and St Alfege, Greenwich, the rebuilding of Eaton Socon church (Beds) after a fire, new furnishings in York Minster, and the remarkable wartime church like a great medieval barn at Greenford, west London. He was a doughty fighter for what he thought right, in particular the recovery of many churches of St Albans Diocese from a state of neglect.

The third name deserving special mention is John Betjeman.[7] As his recently published letters have shown, his distrust of narrow antiquarianism made him at first dismissive of the Council and its works. Thus, although he had been happy to enlist FCE's support in 1939 against some changes to Uffington church, he wrote in 1943 to John Piper that he thought Comper could be persuaded to lend a drawing to the exhibition *The Artist and the*

FIG 21 *John Betjeman sitting on the platform of Broad Street Station clutching his papers for the CCC Executive Committee meeting in January 1972. (Photograph by Snowdon.)*

Church which Piper was organising and which, ironically, the Council had commended, because 'when he understands that it is to do in Eeles and Maufe, he will probably come round'.[8] In November 1949 he wrote to Sir George Barnes, who had sought his advice about establishing a central advisory body, that there already was one but that 'Dr Eeles and Miss Scott, who run the Central Council, are primarily antiquarians and cataloguers, and not people whose aesthetic judgement we would think of seeking'.[9] However, he had already become intrigued by FCE's single-minded enthusiasm, and captivated by JDGS's charm. He visited Dunster in August 1946 and afterwards wrote, in that disarmingly mocking style which he used towards others whom he admired, such as Comper:

> I do not believe I ever wrote to thank you for your and Miss Scott's kind welcome to me at Dunster. *I am certainly coming again.* And I will take Miss Scott to the cinema so that she will be able to clear some of those rood lofts out of her mind. And I will take you too because after one has been to an American film one realises how beautiful England still is, despite its wires and prefabs and tin signs and road houses and motor cars ...

> The Queen was in the kitchen
> > Washing up the bowls
> The King was in the cellar
> > Shovelling the coals
> The Maid was in the garden
> > Eating bread and honey
> And talking to a neighbour
> > About getting more money

I believe the Dean of Durham wrote that. I thought you might like it.[10]
The point of the parody is that the Dean of Durham was Cyril Alington, who was famed for the ease with which he could turn out beautiful hymnody which sounded as though one had heard it before without quite knowing where. One wonders how such a letter was received in Dunster. By 1956 Betjeman had become a Council member, and was concerned enough to write the letter to JDGS which has already been quoted, and in 1961 he gave the Council all Sir Charles Nicholson's drawings, which are now at the RIBA Drawings Collection. When JDGS retired he wrote that 'you continued what Dr Eeles began and, as he would have wished, you made it greater'.[11] As he grew older and Parkinson's disease began to make descent into the All Hallows crypt for meetings increasingly difficult, he came less frequently. But he attended one where, with a well-timed interjection he persuaded the Council to support the view of a delegation which had advised against an architect's scheme for radical alteration to a medieval church in Buckinghamshire even while the architect was sitting at the table. After one of the meetings in the crypt in the early 1970s he left behind his agenda inscribed with the hitherto unpublished verse:

> I'm here at the bottom of a hole in New York City
> > I'm here at the bottom of a hole and can't get out
> I'm here at the bottom of a hole in New York City
> > It's death in the afternoon without a doubt.

5
Organisation 1954–96

A TIME OF CHANGE

A review of central Church funds in 1956 proposed a reorganisation of the boards of Church Assembly which was not in the end adopted. This was fortunate for the Council, since one recommendation was that its budget should be cut from £3,920 to £3,000. But the Council decided that another recommendation, to re-form its composition, would be worth implementing. The membership, comprising two representatives appointed by each DAC together with the Church Assembly representatives and a few co-opted members, amounted to the unwieldy total of 106. A smaller membership would be more practical, provided that the Council was given the resources to maintain its contacts with DACs by holding two conferences a year. In June 1958 a new constitution, the first change since 1927, stipulated a Council of 25 members, all appointed by the Standing Committee of Church Assembly. Instead of meeting twice a year, the Council would in future meet monthly, removing the need for a standing committee. To maintain links with DACs, an Annual General Meeting of DAC Chairmen and Secretaries was instituted, the first being held on 22 October 1959, and the Annual Conferences took on greater importance. Although Chairmen of the four principal boards of Church Assembly were *ex officio* members of the Standing Committee, the Council fell into a second category of boards, for which instead a member of the Standing Committee was appointed to attend Council meetings. A new Technical Panel enabled the Council to profit from advice given by some of those who were no longer members, and a Finance Committee was established. The Wallpaintings Committee and Organs Advisory Committee continued, together with a temporary committee compiling a report on parochial libraries.

Further changes in the Council's constitution came about as a result of the establishment of General Synod in place of the Church Assembly in 1970. From this time the chairmen have tended to change more frequently to conform with the Synodical five-year cycle. The chairmen since that date have generally continued the decanal tradition – the late Michael Stancliffe of Winchester (1972–5), Richard Wingfield-Digby of Peterborough (1975–81), and Christopher Campling of Ripon (1988–94) –

though Eric Evans (1981–8) was Archdeacon of Cheltenham and resigned on becoming Dean of St Paul's. The present chairman, Colin Scott (appointed 1994), was a member of the Council and the Executive Committee in the 1970s, and is now the Suffragan Bishop of Hulme in the Diocese of Manchester.

The new Synod brought a new constitution, based on the recommendations of a Places of Worship Commission, and intended to pull together disparate bodies which had grown up over a period of time. It took effect from 11 January 1972. This was the reason for the Council's change of name, against its wishes, to 'Council for Places of Worship', which it remained for almost a decade. The new Council was to meet three times a year to discuss matters of policy, and responsible to it were three major Committees – an Executive Committee to transact casework referred under the Pastoral Measure and the faculty jurisdiction; a Conservation Committee (formed in 1969 out of the Technical Panel and the Wallpaintings Committee) to co-ordinate the work of twelve sub-committees giving specialist advice in all types of church furnishing underpinned by grant aid of £25,000 per annum provided by the Pilgrim Trust; and a New Churches Committee which in 1974 became the Design and Planning Committee. The Council remained outside the four principal boards, though the Chairman was now invited to attend meetings of the Standing Committee of General Synod. But he was not allowed to vote, because the Standing Committee was not convinced that the Council's role was central to the evangelistic work of the Church.

This arrangement continued until 1990 when, for economic reasons and because the separation of casework from policy proved to be unsatisfactory, the Executive Committee was abolished and the Council again combined the transaction of casework with discussion of policy. The Design and Planning Committee also vanished. More recently, a joint committee has been established with English Heritage to investigate matters of common concern in the conservation field, and the specialist conservation committees have been reduced in number to seven.

THE SECRETARIES

JDGS launched a number of new initiatives, particularly the establishment of conferences to assist discussions between the Council and DACs and between the Council and other bodies such as the Royal Institute of British Architects (RIBA), the Ecclesiastical Architects' and Surveyors'

Association (EASA) and the newer Conference on the Training of Architects in Conservation (COTAC) and the Standing Joint Conference on Natural Stone (SJCNS). She represented the Council's interest on the committees and councils of many other societies, particularly the Society of Antiquaries, the SPAB, ICOMOS, the Society of British Master Glass Painters, HCPT, the Incorporated Church Building Society and the Corpus Vitrearum Medii Aevi. Her achievement was recognised by an OBE in 1970, but in the following year, in June 1971, she was advised by her doctors that she must retire at the early age of 54. She moved almost as far from London as possible, to Buckie on the Moray Firth, but continued to take an interest in church affairs, not least by serving as a member of the Advisory Board for Redundant Churches 1973–80, and involved herself in Scottish conservation issues.

To succeed her as Secretary, a retired civil servant, Desmond Mandeville (DCM), was appointed. He held a double first in the Natural Science Tripos at Cambridge, and had served as a missionary in India before the war and later as Scientific Officer in the Ministry of Defence and the Overseas Development Department, travelling widely in this country and abroad, especially in Asia, until his retirement in 1970 when he was made an OBE. One of his more intrepid mountaineering adventures was the ascent of Mount Ararat to view, not Noah's Ark, but the possible launching of Russian rockets from pads across the border, a mission which understandably remained secret, except to his family, for much of his life. His term of office, which ran from September 1971 until May 1977, was marked by his secretaryship of the working party on state aid for historic churches in use, and by the preparation of a report to General Synod, entitled *Treasures on Earth*, which incorporated his ingenious scheme for declaring items of church plate redundant on the analogy of the procedure for closing churches. On a more mundane level, his scientific background stood him in good stead when the Council was asked to establish guidelines to accompany the Parochial Registers and Records Measure 1978 setting out the appropriate environmental standards for a safe to be used by those parishes which wished to retain their records. Retiring from the Council at the age of 66 he became Secretary of the Art Workers Guild, and in 1991 at the age of 80, he enrolled for an Open University course on the Augustan Age of Rome. It was characteristic of his breadth of interest that he should have been a founder member of the International Guild of Knot Tiers in 1982 and that, in spite of his desk-bound office years, he should have found time to glide, ski, walk, canoe and climb mountains.

During Mandeville's time there was also a tremendous increase in the volume of casework which the Council was statutorily obliged to transact both under the Pastoral Measure 1968, not only in the number of cases but in the greater comprehensiveness of the reports which the Council was required to prepare, and under the rules accompanying the Faculty Jurisdiction Measure 1964. This, together with the expanding work of advice and grant-giving undertaken by the Conservation Committee and its sub-committees, led to a gradual increase in staff. During the Council's time at All Hallows, both Christopher Bourne and David Bishop, his successor as Guild Vicar, shared in the Council's work. By 1970 the staff numbered seven and by 1975 it had risen to twelve and a half, although in that year economies had to be made and it was reduced to ten. Two years later, in 1977, after several years in which the Pastoral Measure work had sometimes exceeded 100 cases per annum, the number was eight full-time, two half-time and three part-time secretaries. The present complement, including three who work for the Cathedrals Fabric Commission, is 15.

On 17 September 1974 the Countess of Dartmouth, Chairman of the Executive Committee of the UK Council for European Architectural Heritage Year 1975, addressed the Council about increasing public awareness of the international importance of our built heritage. The Council's contribution was in two parts. It organised, in co-operation with the Ecclesiastical Architects' and Surveyors' Association, a travelling exhibition, *Caring for Churches*, which was opened at St Andrew, Holborn by Lady Birk, Parliamentary Under Secretary of State for the Heritage at the Department of the Environment, on 2 April 1975, and toured the country throughout the year; and, with the Standing Conference for Local History (now the British Association for Local History), it co-ordinated a church guide book competition, the prizes from 560 entries being awarded by Sir John Betjeman and Professor Asa Briggs. A second church guide book competition, for which Lord Briggs was again a judge, was held in 1983 and noted amongst the 753 entries a considerable improvement in presentation, especially among the leaflets.

Having been Secretary of the Cathedrals Advisory Commission since June 1976, Peter Burman became Secretary of the Council on 1 May 1977; David Williams was appointed Assistant, later Deputy, Secretary, and on his move in 1986 to the Central Board of Finance, of which he is now Secretary, he was succeeded by Jonathan Goodchild.

In the autumn of 1977 Dr Roy Strong, Director of the V&A, put on a sequel to the exhibition *The Destruction of the Country House* which had so dramatically drawn attention to the plight of many historic buildings. Entitled *Change and Decay: the Future of Our Churches*, it was organised by Peter Burman with Marcus Binney, then Architectural Editor of *Country Life*, and was intended, while stressing the problems, to offer positive ideas about how they might be resolved and to press the Government for a starting date for state aid for historic churches. It was accompanied by an illustrated book[1] with essays by several Council and DAC members which emphasised the richness of the heritage of buildings and furnishings. The organisers also published a report, *Churches and Chapels: Who Cares*, commissioned by the British Tourist Authority, which contained facts and figures relating to English churches and cathedrals and much new material on Free Church architecture in Scotland and Wales as well as England.

In the same year Marcus Binney addressed the Council on the subject of churches and tourism, and a working party was established to open discussions with the English Tourist Board. In 1981 the Council presented a report, *Churches and Tourism*, to Synod which aroused considerable interest and organised a conference of the same title in association with the University of Bristol. Since then several other initiatives have been pursued, and the Council hopes that the Open Churches Trust recently established by Sir Andrew Lloyd Webber will also help to make more churches accessible to visitors.

As a result of lay inheritance of what until the Reformation had been the rector's responsibilities for the repair of chancels of parish churches, many individuals and organisations remain financially liable for such repairs. Sometimes the obligation is vested in a body such as an Oxford or Cambridge college, sometimes in the patron of the living or sometimes even, perhaps unknown to the unwary purchaser, in a parcel of ground in the parish. The question of abolishing this liability, which has been seen as unfair, has been raised from time to time, most pressingly in 1977, when it was reckoned that 6,030 churches had chancel repair liability vested in someone other than the PCC. A CCC working party investigated the matter and concluded that it should be abolished over a period of time, perhaps with commutation payments in special cases. But despite the impetus of a report from the Law Commission, nothing has yet been implemented.

Peter Burman resigned the Secretaryship at the end of January 1990 to become Director of Conservation Studies at the Institute of Advanced Architectural Studies in the University of York. The Annual Report paid warm tribute to the 'energy, enthusiasm and experience' which he had brought to the Council's work during a period of more than 20 years and he was made MBE. He did much to build up contacts with kindred bodies, to promote a better understanding of conservation in churches and to encourage young artists and craftsmen to work for the Church. He was responsible, with others, for two major exhibitions, the enlarged edition of the *Churchyards Handbook*, for continuing the negotiations towards the introduction of state aid for historic churches and for a number of extra-mural projects supported by the Council such as the Friends of Christ Church, Spitalfields.

His successor, Dr Thomas Cocke, the present Secretary, came to the Council from the Royal Commission on Historical Monuments, where his work included published studies of the churches of Northamptonshire and south-east Wiltshire as well as the building history of Salisbury Cathedral and the houses of the Close. Educated at Marlborough College and Pembroke College, Cambridge and trained at the Courtauld Institute, he was no stranger to the Council, having been for some years a member of the CCC Executive Committee, the Advisory Board for Redundant Churches and the St Edmundsbury and Ipswich DAC.

The scrupulous administration of grants allocated from funds provided by the Pilgrim Trust and other charitable bodies requires much correspondence about matters of detail with parishes, conservators, and expert advisers in order to ensure that the work is carried out to the highest standards and in a proper order of priority. In 1964 an Administrative Officer was appointed, chiefly to correspond with wallpaintings conservators. Since then the conservation work has been administered by nine successive officers with their assistants, and the present holder of the post is Andrew Argyrakis. Moreover, in order to cope with the rapid increase of casework referred under the Pastoral Measure 1968, which came into operation on 1 April 1969, another member of staff was taken on. After Neil Burton, now Secretary of the Georgian Group, Donald Findlay was appointed in August 1973 and has carried out this work to the present, visiting and compiling reports on all churches where the future is under review.

THE LIBRARY

On the Council's arrival at Fulham Palace it was recognised that the library, based on FCE's collection of topographical books given in 1937, was a resource which ought to be made available to members of the public, and Joan Petersen was appointed Librarian. She and her successors – Basil Fairclough, who had been appointed Exhibitions Officer, but combined this with the library work and the complete reorganisation of the Council's filing system, David Williams and Janet Seeley – have had to answer many and varied questions over the years in addititon to supervising visiting students and researchers. Miss Petersen gave much help to authors such as John Betjeman with the *Collins Guide to English Parish Churches* and Peter Anson with *Fashions in Church Furnishings*, books which have become classics. She also helped Big Chief I-Spy with the compilation of *I Spy Churches*, which sold over 100,000 copies and must have alerted untold numbers of children to the fascination of historic churches.

The library holdings are augmented by a modest annual purchase grant and by copies of books reviewed in *Churchscape*, and have been much enriched over the years by bequests of books and other material from Will Croome, Basil Clarke, Gordon Barnes and others. The library also holds copies of all the inventories prepared by Church Recorders Groups of the National Association of Decorative and Fine Arts Societies and detailed records of the conservation of objects carried out with grant aid allocated by the Council, to assist conservators working on them in the future. The Council continues to make its library and information in the files of the national survey of churches available to members of the public by appointment.

LINKS WITH DIOCESAN ADVISORY COMMITTEES

The Council's co-ordination of DAC work has remained a top priority. The CCC Conferences, having been at first limited to DAC Chairmen and Secretaries, soon became annual events, open to all DAC members from 1957 and gradually more widely attended not only by DAC members but also by members of kindred organisations. They were held in either Oxford or Cambridge for some years, but ventured into the provinces in 1963 when, the Oxbridge colleges being unavailable, the conference was based at Wills Hall, Bristol. Later it went to St John's College, York, and it has since been held in various dioceses, ranging from Exeter in the south-west to Norwich in the east and Carlisle in the north. Over the years its organisation has increasingly become a joint effort between the Council and the local DAC. The Council has also arranged occasional conferences on particular topics such as bells, stained glass, churchyards, church inspection and repair, tourism and wallpaintings.

Many other topics have been covered by publications, as listed in Appendix 2, and by articles in the annual review (now called *Churchscape*). The provision of facilities in churches for the disabled, for example, was first discussed in an article in October 1964. In the following year it was again brought to the attention of DACs in the Newsletter. 1981 was the International Year of Disabled Persons, and many churches have since installed hearing loops for the deaf and improved access and toilet facilities for the physically disabled. Such matters as the conflict of sloping lines of ramps with the rectilinear design of church steps have caused considerable problems for DACs, though they are aware of the vital need for the disabled to have equal access to churches.

FACULTY JURISDICTION

The Faculty Jurisdiction Measure 1938 had been a noble attempt in its time, but it was increasingly found to be lacking in several areas, not least by its omission of any mention of the CCCC. The Council had no right to give evidence at consistory court hearings (where held) into the sale of valuables, and indeed could find that entire churches had been demolished without its knowledge. On the other hand, demolition of churches under the Reorganisation Areas Measure obliged the Church Commissioners to seek the Council's advice in every case. In evidence submitted to the Commission chaired by Lord Bridges which was established in 1960 to review the Measure, the Council suggested amongst other things that demolition of churches by faculty should be severely restricted and that, where such cases occurred, both the DAC and the CCCC should be consulted (which was put into the Faculty Jurisdiction Measure 1964). The Council also proposed that a model DAC constitution should be framed (which did not happen until the Care of Churches and Ecclesiastical Jurisdiction Measure 1991).

In recognition of the introduction in 1977 of state aid for historic churches in use, the Church agreed to review its supervisory and monitoring system. This work was carried out by the Faculty Jurisdiction Commission which sat from 1980 to 1984 under the chairmanship of the Bishop of Chichester, with the CCC member Martin Caroe amongst its number, Peter Burman as an assessor and Donald Findlay as one of the two Assistant Secretaries. Its report, *The Continuing Care of Churches and Cathedrals*, led to the Care of Churches and Ecclesiastical Jurisdiction Measure 1991 which improved on the Faculty Jurisdiction Measure 1964 by clarifying many obscurities and formulating, for example, precise models for the constitution and membership of DACs, elucidating the role of churchwardens in maintaining inventories and regularly monitoring the condition of their churches, giving archdeacons special powers of intervention, and for the first time formally involving English Heritage and the statutory amenity societies (the Council for British Archaeology, the Ancient Monuments Society, the Society for the Protection of Ancient Buildings, the Georgian Group, the Victorian Society and, later, the Twentieth Century Society) in the appointment of DAC members and in faculty procedure.

The Council's involvement in faculty jurisdiction casework has steadily grown over the years. From 1993 to 1995 the total number of cases almost doubled from 67 to 115. As well as covering proposed sales of objects from churches, the faculty casework has shown a great increase in the number of projected extensions to churches, which has elicited statements from the Royal Fine Art Commission and the SPAB and booklets published by two dioceses, by English Heritage and, most recently, by the Council itself. Re-ordering of church interiors, both for liturgical reasons and to provide better facilities such as lavatories and kitchens, which might have astonished early Council members, are also increasing and are covered in the Council's booklet. Many of these proposals demand site visits if the Council is to offer realistic advice, and the Council is deeply grateful to those people, both Council members and external experts, who are prepared to give their time and talents to this work.

THE CHURCH AND THE ARTIST:
THE EXHIBITION YEARS

During the 1950s the Council had become increasingly aware of the subject of new churches and new art within existing churches. Before the war it had been tempted to dismiss works of art in churches as irrelevant because they fulfilled no liturgical function. But increasingly churches wanted to install modern windows, sculptured figures and other non-liturgical objects which might inspire thought, devotion or contemplation outside services.

The CCCC Conferences of 1957 and 1958 included lectures on modern art, and a travelling exhibition, *The Church and the Artist*, organised by the CCCC staff, which included photographs of sculpture, textiles and stained glass by, amongst others, Sir Jacob Epstein, Sir Charles Wheeler, John Piper,

FIG 22 *Memorial tablet to a two-year-old child in Skipwith Church, Yorkshire, designed by Laurence Whistler and executed by Cecil Thomas, 1956–7. Included in a CCC exhibition as an example of good design and lettering in a traditional style. (Photograph in CCC collection.)*

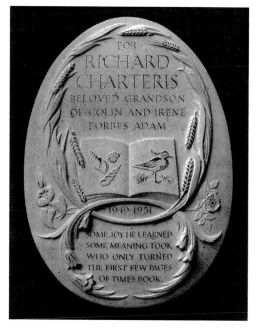

Erwin Bossanyi and Louis Osman, was so popular that it ran over from one year to the next. The Council stated that it wished to encourage boldness rather than 'a safe Diocesan Advisory Committee style'.

In February 1959 the Council was asked by the Chancellor of the Diocese of York to consider Sir Jacob Epstein's offer of his sculpture *Ecce Homo*, a figure 11 ft high which he had carved in c.1935, to Selby Abbey.[2] The gift was commended by the York DAC, and G.G. Pace, the architect to the Abbey, had decided to locate it at the east end of the south choir aisle. But a CCCC delegation thought that it would look better in the north transept. Pace explained that the reason for the south aisle position was that the statue was work of religious art and should not be visible during divine service, as it would be in the north transept. A compromise location under the north-west tower was agreed. But the vicar objected because that would hinder large baptisms. In the end there were local objections, and the chancellor refused the faculty lest the statue should lead to dissension within the parish.

During the 1960s the Council used All Hallows, London Wall as a Christian Art Centre, holding exhibitions intended to encourage those responsible for churches to appreciate the virtues of new art forms. The first

FIG 23 *Christopher Bourne, guild vicar of All Hallows, London Wall, seen at the door of the church with a vamping horn from the exhibition* The Church Gallery Minstrels *(1963).* *(Photograph by Keystone Press Agency, Ltd.)*

FIG 24 *All Hallows, London Wall, during the exhibition* Designs for Stained Glass *(1965).* *(Photograph by Sydney W. Newbery.)*

FIG 25 *The Captivity window, from a pair depicting Captivity and Freedom installed in Broxted Church, Essex, to designs by John Clark to commemorate the Beirut hostages, 1993. John McCarthy's father sought advice on the choice of an artist from the CCC and selected Mr Clark from the examples of his work in the files. (Photograph by John K. Clark.)*

Exhibitions Officer was Basil Fairclough, the Council's librarian, who held
the post from 1962 until early 1967. He was followed by John Gordon
Christian, William Young and Anthony Symondson. The first exhibition,
The Craftsman and his Craft, which featured craftsmen at work, was held in
July 1962, and during the next ten years over eighty exhibitions were held.
Three, in 1962, 1964 and 1969, were devoted to new churches and, in the
case of the second, the creation of new churches from old. Other topics
included *The Church Gallery Minstrels* (1963), *The Parson Through the Eyes
of* Punch (1964) and *London Transport Posters* (1971). Several exhibitions
broke new ground in the study of antiquarian subjects, most importantly
those devoted to *English Monumental Sculpture* (1964, organised with the
help of the V&A, Rupert Gunnis and photographs from the National
Buildings Record), *Organs in British Churches* (1967, organised by Michael
Gillingham and John Gordon Christian), *English Mediaeval Wallpaintings*
(1968) and *Victorian and Edwardian Ecclesiastical Design* (1967, sponsored by
the Victorian Society) with a catalogue by Anthony Symondson which,
with a parallel exhibition of plate at Goldsmiths Hall, prefigured the
influential Victorian Church Art exhibition at the V&A in 1971. Modern
artists who had one-man shows included Sir Jacob Epstein (1963), Susan
Glyn (1966), Rodney Hubbuck (1967), and David Peace (1968). In
addition, the BBC used All Hallows for filming its weekly religious
programme *Seeing is Believing*.

The contacts established by the exhibitions encouraged the Council to
begin keeping records of working artists and craftsmen together with
illustrations of their work. Although with the increase of other areas of the
Council's work during the 1970s these valuable assets fell rather into the
background, Peter Burman was keen to encourage artists willing to carry out
work for churches and, in particular, to add the names of promising young
artists to the Council's lists. They are now kept up to date so that parishes
can seek advice about artists and craftsmen working for the church over a
wide range of fields. Peter Burman was also involved in the organisation of
an exhibition *Prophecy and Vision*, held in Bristol in 1982 and accompanied
by an illustrated catalogue which publicised the church work of many
artists. The exhibition was held in association with the first conference 'The
Creative Artist and the Church', which has now become an annual event,
intended to promote a closer understanding between artists and the church.

6
Furnishings and conservation

Wallpaintings

The Council had taken an interest in the care and repair (as it was then called) of church furnishings since its earliest days – in 1926 it had organised a conference on wallpaintings – but it was only after the war that the Council's experience of work in the conservation field brought about a transformation. Until that time, although the country's greatest collections of art objects such as wallpaintings, stained glass and sculpture are found in our churches, almost all conservators were confined within museum and gallery laboratories. It seemed as though the two could not be brought together, until the formation in 1953 of a Wallpaintings Committee under the joint auspices of the Council and the SPAB, with Will Croome as its first chairman. The members included the architects John Macgregor (representing the SPAB), W.H. Randoll Blacking and Robert Potter, the conservators Dr H.J. Plenderleith and Professor Robert Baker, and the antiquary Dr Geoffrey Bushnell. The Committee immediately began consultations with experts in Denmark, Germany and Belgium and with all the practitioners in England. Museum conservators began to realise that objects from churches would be returned to environments which did not conform to museum conditions, and, indeed, that work on some types of object would have to be carried out *in situ*.

What little conservation work had been done in churches had sometimes proved unsuccessful. *The Conservation of English Wallpaintings*, the Committee's report published in 1959 was the outcome of research and discussion both in this country and abroad. It broke new ground by giving a comprehensive account of the methods used by medieval painters and a review of the different methods of conservation. It laid down definitive, scientifically justifiable recommendations for what should be done in the future. It showed that the problems of British wallpaintings were unique because of the dampness of our climate compared with other countries rich in wallpaintings; that, although moisture could not be eliminated from ancient walls, it could at least evaporate continually if they were kept healthy; and that the treatment of wallpaintings by the late Victorians and their successors, sealing them with varnish or wax, together with extensive repainting of lost areas, though providing initially delightful results, bright in colour and clear to decipher, had proved disastrous in the longer term, retaining water within the wall until in the worst cases it could blow the painting off the surface. In less dramatic cases the wax had darkened until it was almost black, with water breaking through cracks in white efflorescence.

A solution was found by Robert and Eve Baker,[1] whose work on wallpaintings in English churches and cathedrals, generously supported by the Pilgrim Trust, transformed them once more into objects of beauty. They found ways of treating surfaces which intervened as little as possible, and with almost magical skill they discovered how to remove one layer of

FIG 26 A & B *The church at Little Witchingham, Norfolk, as it was in 1973. Wallpaintings were discovered under many layers of whitewash by Eve Baker in 1967, the fabric was repaired in the early 1970s with grants from the Norfolk Churches Trust and the wallpaintings, which proved to survive in a remarkably complete state, were conserved by the Perry Lithgow Partnership between 1975 and 1986 at a cost of about £22,350 contributed by the Pilgrim Trust, the Hayward Foundation and the Radcliffe Trust (all through the CCC) and by the Department of the Environment and, subsequently, English Heritage. The lower photograph shows the lion emblem of St Mark on a spandrel of the nave arcade, uncovered and conserved in 1982. The church is now vested in the Churches Conservation Trust. (Photographs by National Monuments Record and Eastern Daily Press.)*

painting to another part of the wall in order to reveal earlier paintings below. Their skills convinced the Committee that they were the only possible practitioners in this country, and so they remained for some years. By 1971, 12 years later, the Committee had supervised a systematic programme of repair, carried out by the Bakers and a few others such as Clive Rouse, to the most important wallpaintings in need of attention at a cost of £85,000 met by the Pilgrim Trust.

Painted woodwork

The Conservation Committee then turned to the next most pressing problem, the conservation of painted woodwork. This was represented especially by painted screens in East Anglia and Devon, of which it was estimated there were 80 in Norfolk alone. Other artists have since taken up the task and, although Eve Baker died in 1990 and Robert Baker died in 1992, their work continues at the hands of conservators fully aware that they must constantly be adapting and improving their techniques to ensure that the methods used are as non-interventionist as possible. Over the years the Pilgrim Trust, which remains the largest provider of funds to the Council's conservation work, has been joined by other trusts such as the Radcliffe Trust, the Hayward Foundation, the Baring Foundation and the Esmée Fairbairn Trust, in addition to private trusts which seek the Council's advice on grant applications.

The Council has continued to encourage the improvement of the skills and techniques of conservators and to persuade parishes to take a positive interest in the care of the objects in their possession. Thus a seminar on sculpture conservation was held at the Art Workers Guild in 1979, an international seminar on wallpainting conservation, involving British and continental practitioners, at Farnham Castle and St Catherine's College, Oxford, later in the same year, and a symposium on monumental effigies at the Tower of London in September 1978.

Stained glass

The Pilgrim Trust was also a crucial factor in the development of stained glass conservation. The historic association of the glazier's craft with York Minster had gained fresh impetus under Dean Milner-White in the years after the Second World War, when the glass which had been removed from the windows was re-instated, much of it being rearranged to eliminate the jumble caused by earlier attempts at repairs. After the completion of this work, and the Dean's death in 1963, the Pilgrim Trustees joined the Dean and Chapter to create the York Glaziers Trust, with the intention that it should carry out conservation of glass from all over the country. Since that time the Trust has conserved many of the country's notable windows, and other conservators have established themselves, carrying out work with grant aid from the Pilgrim Trust channelled through the CCC.

Organs

Although the Council had published a memorandum on the placing of organs in churches in 1929, it was anxiety about what might happen to English organs in the reconstruction of churches after the war which encouraged Cecil Clutton in 1942 to form a committee to offer advice on this subject. It was re-formed in 1953, the same year as the founding of the Wallpaintings Committee, as the Organs Advisory Committee of the CCCC under the Chairmanship of Sir William McKie, organist of Westminster Abbey, with Cecil Clutton and Austin Niland as Joint Honorary Secretaries. Sam Clutton (1909–91), as he was always called, was the sixth generation to serve in the family firm of surveyors, a remarkable character of extraordinary and single-minded energy with three principal areas of interest – clocks, vintage cars and organs – to all of which he brought a vigorous and fearless advocacy, and about each of which he published at least one book. He never minded what he said, and in writing to FCE about the establishment of the Organs Advisory Committee he claimed that what the average parish organist knew about organs could be thinly spread on a sixpenny bit. His passion for organs was well in advance of its time, looking back beyond the nineteenth-century school of organ playing which still prevailed in the 1930s to the works of J.S. Bach and the instruments on which he played them. Clutton accordingly promoted the revival of the classical organ, but he also did much to ensure that historic English organs were appreciated and preserved, beginning with that at Adlington Hall, Cheshire, upon which Handel played. The Committee's original members were the architect Stephen Dykes Bower, his brother John (Organist of St Paul's Cathedral, who later became Chairman), Dr Francis Jackson (Organist of York Minster), the Revd Noel Boston, Gerald Knight (Director of the Royal School of Church Music) and the organbuilders Cuthbert Harrison and Herbert Norman. Later Lionel Dakers, Michael Gillingham and others joined the Committee, the former being its Chairman from 1975 until 1996; Donald Findlay was its clerk from 1975 until 1989. From about 1970 the Committee's advisory work has been reinforced by the allocation of grants towards the conservation of historic organs from the funds made available to the Council by the Pilgrim Trust and other bodies.

The Organs Advisory Committee held occasional one-day conferences for Diocesan Organs Advisers in the 1950s and 1960s, and during the 1970s the conferences became residential, moving about the country like the main CCC Conference. In 1962 the Committee's attempt to prepare a list of organbuilders categorised according to their skills and abilities went badly wrong when the list was inadvertently sent out to all the organbuilders before it had been finalised. Another crisis was averted in 1969 when Lady Jeans, the scholar of historic organs, published an article, 'The Baroquising of English Organs' which accused Diocesan Organs Advisers and the Organs Advisory Committee of ignoring Continental research and instead advocating the addition of unsuitable Baroque sections to English Romantic organs. A delegation from the Committee was able to persuade Lady Jeans that this was something which the Committee had in fact always abhorred. The question of electronic organs has also exercised the Committee for many years.

Monuments

In addition to allocating grant aid for the conservation of many medieval monuments and brasses, the Council soon became anxious about the over-enthusiastic recolouring of seventeenth-century monuments, many of which

FIG 27 *Oak effigy of a knight, c.1320, at Ashwell, Leics, conserved in 1991 by Harrison Hill Ltd with grant aid allocated by the CCC. (Photograph by Harrison Hill Ltd.)*

FIG 28 *Monument by Sir Henry Cheere erected by Mary Martin to commemorate members of her family at Netteswell, Essex, in c.1765. Shown as it was in 1944, the monument was later badly treated after the closure of the church, and partly dismantled. The components were rescued and the monument is now on display in the English Sculpture Gallery at the V&A. The church was declared redundant in 1978 and is now a house. (Photograph by W.D. Clark.)*

had been gaudily repainted. This made them bright and cheerful but obscured or even destroyed evidence of their original colouring. The leading figure in their appreciation was Mrs Katharine Esdaile (1881–1950), who published several books and numerous articles on post-medieval sculpture. Another protagonist for post-Reformation sculptured monuments, and especially the Baroque and neo-classical work of the eighteenth century, was Rupert Gunnis (1899–1965), a member of the CCCC and CAC and Chairman of both Canterbury and Rochester DACs, who lived near Tunbridge Wells but just as frequently wrote letters from impressive addresses such as Stratfield Saye or Castle Howard where he happened to be staying. His *Dictionary of British Sculptors 1660-1851*, embodying the fruit of many years of research and of visiting churches and houses, transformed the public awareness of this subject. In 1964 he suggested that the V&A should establish a gallery of English post-Renaissance sculpture, which enabled the Museum to rescue and display valuable monuments at risk in derelict churches such as Netteswell, Essex and Eastwell, Kent. When he died in the next year he left the CCCC £5,000. The interest from this amount is still applied in grants for the conservation of church and cathedral monuments within the period 1660–1860. Gunnis imparted his enthusiasm to John Physick, who has long been a member of the Monuments Sub-Committee of the CCC and latterly Chairman of the Conservation Committee.

Parochial libraries

In September 1959 the Council published a major report entitled *The Parochial Libraries of the Church of England*, compiled in response to a request from the Archbishops ten years before. The report, principally the work of F.C. Morgan and Neil Ker, contains a historical introduction, an alphabetical list of libraries past and present and some advice on the care of ancient books. Attention was drawn to regrettable instances where libraries had been thrown away or burnt as being old and neglected, or accidentally dispersed on the death of an incumbent or the sale of a parsonage house. Wishing to avoid the recurrence of a case such as Shipdham, Norfolk, where the parochial library had been sold in 1947 without reference to the DAC or CCCC on the grounds that the chancellor did not consider that the library came within the scope of the DAC's concern, the Council pressed for the revised Faculty Jurisdiction Measure to make it clear that it was proper for chancellors to consult DACs about libraries. A suitable clause was incorporated in the Measure when it was enacted in 1964. The 1959 report is currently being revised by Michael Perkin.

Communion plate and valuables

About 1960 there was increasing anxiety that, in order to pay for the repairs being specified by architects as a result of the systematic inspection of churches, parishes were more frequently considering the sale of treasures, especially plate stored in banks, instead of discovering other ways of raising money. One, for example, had been intending to sell a seventeenth-century flagon before applying to the Historic Churches Preservation Trust. The CCCC felt that there was widespread misunderstanding amongst the clergy about the use of flagons and that 'many who would not dream of selling a chalice have no scruples about selling a flagon, on the grounds that it had not held the Sacred Elements'. But, the CCCC pointed out, wine was often consecrated in flagons in accordance with the Prayer Book rubric, so they were just as much sacramental vessels as chalices and patens. It was hoped that, in cases where a faculty was granted, the sale could be restricted to

FIG 29 *Communion cup of unusual form and decoration by Robert Williamson of York, 1664, from Londesborough, Yorks, conserved by H.C. Fowler in 1993 with grant aid from the Worshipful Company of Goldsmiths. (Photograph by the Worshipful Company of Goldsmiths.)*

another church or a museum.

An appeal judgement[2] delivered in the Court of the Arches by the Deputy Dean concerning the sale of two flagons from Tredington, Warwickshire, in 1970, set a precedent for the consideration of future faculty petitions for the sale of valuables. It reversed the decision of the diocesan chancellor not to allow the sale because, the Deputy Dean felt, the petitioners had satisfactorily proved two things – that the items were redundant and that the parish was facing a financial crisis in the care of its building. Later, the same judge, sitting as Chancellor of the Diocese of London in the case of the proposed sale of plate from St Mary le Bow,[3] was to add a third criterion, namely that the chancellor might consider granting a faculty where a parish could prove that it required the proceeds to carry out a special ministry.

While parishes might look on plate merely as a financial asset which they might liquidate, sales were also proposed because they were embarrassed by valuable silver sitting unused either in vestry safes or in bank vaults. Only a few took up the Council's suggestion that valuable plate might at least be displayed on the altar at festivals because of the practical difficulties involved in collecting and returning the plate, apart from the risk of theft. One solution, warmly welcomed by the Council, was the establishment in cathedrals of treasuries for the public display of plate from parishes in the diocese, sponsored by the Worshipful Company of Goldsmiths. The first of these was set up at Lincoln in 1960, followed by those at Winchester and Norwich. The scheme was later extended to a number of other cathedrals such as Peterborough, Gloucester and Durham.

In 1970 the Council reported that in the 40 cases of faculty applications for the sale of church plate which had come to its notice over the previous 26 years, chancellors had refused faculties in only four, and noted that there was inconsistency of practice between one diocese and another. There were also reports of dealers going round parishes encouraging them to sell plate by identifying it as secular, which the CCC found especially frustrating when it was not called to give evidence which would prove them wrong.

A Council working party produced a report, *Treasures on Earth*, for debate in Synod in 1973 which reiterated the Council's long-held view that valuable possessions should be insured not for full replacement value (which could probably never be achieved) but for the cost of a good craftsman-made modern replacement. It also set out a scheme, devised by Desmond Mandeville, for declaring individual items of plate redundant. The first proposal met with approval from Synod, but the second was thought to be too intricate, and it was decided that the merits of proposals for selling plate should continued to be tested by hearings in consistory courts as before.

A spate of thefts of arms and armour from churches encouraged the Council in 1967 to carry out an inventory of these objects by archdeaconry, the results of which enabled an assessment to be made of the relative quality and distribution of surviving examples.

Bells

In February 1954 the Church Assembly approved by a large majority a resolution moved by Ivor Bulmer-Thomas deprecating the 'introduction into churches of recordings of bells and instruments simulating the sound of bells'. In 1959 an agreement about the proper treatment of historic bells, hammered out between the Council's Bells Sub-Committee, representatives of bellringers and the two firms of bellfounders, was embodied in a published code of practice which, with subsequent revisions, remains in operation today. The CCC also encouraged a small group to experiment with preserving cracked bells by welding, which saved many of them from the melting pot.

Registers and records

The Society of Genealogists proposed, and the Council agreed, in 1970, that parish registers and records, hitherto kept in safes in church vestries or wherever the churchwardens thought fit, should be deposited with Diocesan Record Offices unless suitable conditions could be provided in the parish church. These proposals were eventually enshrined in the Parochial Registers and Records Measure 1978, which required Diocesan Record Offices to survey the parish registers and records in their area and take all those over 100 years old into their care unless the parish could meet stringent requirements about the environment in which they would retain them. The CCC prepared the guidelines for a safe which would provide the best climatic conditions, and the guide which accompanied the measure.

CHURCHYARDS

In 1960 the Council commended to other dioceses the example of an anonymous donation of £1,000 made to the Bishop of Gloucester to establish a fund offering small grants for the preservation of the table tombs typical of the diocese. Perhaps as a result, the Council, having for years tried to persuade parishes to tidy up their churchyards, resolved that it would oppose indiscriminate clearance of churchyards, and that monuments dating from the seventeenth to the early nineteenth century should remain *in situ* unless badly broken or completely illegible. In 1970 the Council declared its opposition to perspex tombstones.

The Council's *Churchyards Handbook*, the largest of its publications hitherto, has run through several editions. With the increasing interest in churchyards as wildlife sanctuaries and repositories of vernacular art and local history, they are being seen as a vital resource. The Council has been involved with organising several conferences on churchyards, notably *Churchyards in the 80s* at Bristol in 1984 and *Wildlife in Churchyards* at the Arthur Rank Centre, Stoneleigh, Warwickshire, in 1995.

7
The inspection and repair
of churches

The recommendations of the report *The Preservation of Our Churches*, introduced to the Church Assembly in 1954 by Ivor Bulmer-Thomas, who had chaired the Commission, became law in the following year as The Inspection of Churches Measure 1955, which obliged every diocese to establish a scheme for the inspection of each church at least once every five years by a suitably qualified architect. Not only did this ensure that the buildings were properly inspected but it created a large enough body of work to allow more architects to specialise in church repair work for the first time. A national scale of recommended fees and panels of recommended architects were agreed with the Royal Institute of British Architects, and the Council remains the Church's negotiator with the RIBA. The CCC prepared a standard format for the log book in which the churchwardens of each parish were encouraged (and, since the Care of Churches and Ecclesiastical Jurisdiction Measure 1991, are obliged) to record works to each church building. Some dioceses were slow to act, but all had a scheme in place by September 1958 when the working of the Measure was reviewed at a conference held at the Institute of Architectural Study in York, attended by over 100 architects. In order to promote the training of architects in the care of old buildings, a subject not thought to be sufficiently covered in the courses accredited by the RIBA, the Council convened a meeting in February 1959, from which arose the Standing Joint Conference on the Recruitment and Training of Architects for the Care of Old Buildings, later renamed the Conference on Training Architects in Conservation (COTAC), with Donald Insall as secretary and JDGS representing the CCCC, to encourage young people interested in old buildings to take up architecture.

The Council was closely involved in the formation in 1969 of two new organisations concerned with the specialist education of architects in the care of old buildings: the Association for the Study of Conservation of Historic Buildings (ASCHB), and the Standing Joint Conference on

Natural Stones (SJCNS) which brought together architects and representatives of the stone trade. The latter organisation also fostered the school of masonry and stone conservation based in a redundant church at Orton near Kettering, Northamptonshire. The Council joined with the RIBA in publishing *Church Inspection and Repair*, launched at a two-day conference at Bedford College, London, in 1970 and which, with revisions, remains in print. In 1971 Dr Derek Linstrum, with the support of the Radcliffe Trust, established mid-career diploma courses in conservation studies at the Institute of Advanced Architectural Studies in York, which continue today.

A proposal made in 1977 that suitably qualified surveyors should be allowed to carry out quinquennial inspections of churches on an equal footing with architects was at first received with some scepticism. In due course the Council was persuaded, and appropriate provision was incorporated in the Care of Churches and Ecclesiastical Jurisdiction Measure 1991. The success of the Church of England's scheme of regular inspection has been such that it has been imitated by other major owners of historic buildings such as the National Trust and the Oxford and Cambridge colleges.

STATE AID FOR HISTORIC CHURCHES

The question of state-funded grants for the repair of historic churches had long been under discussion when the Local Authorities (Historic Buildings) Act 1962 empowered local authorities to give grants or loans to buildings of historic or architectural interest. The possibility of government aid was first publicly mooted in September 1964. In 1971 the Government, though indicating that it had 'an open mind' on the matter, made it clear that, in exchange for government money, churches would be expected to submit to local authority listed building consents for both external and internal works. In response, the July sessions of General Synod that year established a Working Party on State Aid under the chairmanship of the Bishop of Rochester, which saw the project through. The Government proposal that listed building consent would have to be sought for work on churches was withdrawn after the Church offered an assurance that it would review the Faculty Jurisdiction, which was carried out by the Chichester Commission in 1980–4. The Working Party on State Aid continues as a forum for discussions with the Government under the chairmanship of the Bishop of Chester.

On 11 November 1976 Lady Birk, Parliamentary Under-Secretary of State at the Department of the Environment, made a statement setting out the terms on which state aid would be offered for parish churches in use for worship (but not cathedrals). But it was not until 1978 that state aid for churches, set at £1 million at 1973 prices, administered by the Historic Buildings Council (and from 1984 by English Heritage), finally came into being. Applications would only be considered from churches of 'outstanding' architectural interest and had to be counter-signed by the archdeacon to ensure that the parish had declared their resources and to confirm that the diocese would not declare the church redundant in the foreseeable future. The scheme was later extended to cover most of the contents of churches, with the exception of mechanical objects like bells, clocks and organs, and then to cathedrals. The criterion of 'outstanding' has also been widened so that all Grade I and Grade II* churches are now automatically eligible for consideration. Some chancellors contended that one condition of the grants, that future works in grant-aided churches should be submitted to HBC/EH for approval, infringed their judicial authority, but this anxiety was eventually allayed.

Central sources of grant aid have been increased in recent years by the establishment in 1980 of the National Heritage Memorial Fund, which offers substantial grants for conservation of important objects in churches, though not for fabric repairs. In 1995 the situation was transformed by the launch of the National Lottery, the proceeds from which, so far as churches are concerned, can be offered in grants for objects of heritage interest in any churches, not only those listed Grade I or II*. Some work on churches may also qualify for grants from other lottery-funded organisations, such as the Arts Council and the Millennium Commission.

REDUNDANT CHURCHES

In 1956 the Chairman corresponded with the Archbishop of Canterbury about a suggestion that some redundant churches should be taken into guardianship by the Ministry of Works, but this came to nothing. In the same year there was a proposal that the fine classical church of Christ Church, Salford, Manchester,[1] by Thomas Wright, a local architect, should be demolished because of the poor condition of the building and the depopulation of the surrounding area. John Betjeman took an immediate interest, noting that the diocese had sent photographs intended to show the least flattering aspects of the building. At first the matter was to be dealt

Fɪɢ 30 *The dramatic soot-blackened silhouette of Christ Church, Salford, Lancs, designed by Thomas Wright, built in 1830–1 with a steeple added by E.H. Shellard in 1846, and demolished in 1958 against the advice of CCC. (Photograph by Peter Fleetwood Hesketh in CCC collection.)*

with under the Reorganisation Areas Measure, which would have given the CCCC a voice, but it was subsequently transferred to the faculty jurisdiction. The chancellor did not invite the CCCC to give evidence at the consistory court hearing but on 19 September, prompted by an anxious inquiry from the Royal Fine Art Commission, it made strong representations to him, especially about the destruction of several furnishings. But the faculty was granted, and by July 1958 the altar had been burnt in accordance with the terms of the faculty, the fine mahogany pulpit and stone font had been broken up with the chancellor's permission when the contractors found that they could not remove them without damage, and the church was almost gone. The Georgian Group was incensed, Ivor Bulmer-Thomas asked a question in the Church Assembly, and John Betjeman ensured that the church remained in the public memory when he dedicated his *Collins Guide to English Parish Churches* (1958) 'To the memory of ST AGNES', KENNINGTON, 1877, CHRIST CHURCH, SALFORD, 1830, *fine churches of unfashionable date demolished since the war*'.

A petition in 1957 from two parishioners to repair the church of Holnest[2] in Dorset, which had been disused since 1940, led to a consistory court hearing at which Ivor Bulmer-Thomas assisted them to put their case for preservation. The archdeacon opposed it, and JDGS appeared for the CCCC to suggest an intermediate proposal that, since a population of 110 could not be expected to raise funds for the complete restoration of the church, the nave should be unroofed but the chancel and tower should be restored. There the file closes, but the church stands today with all its roofs intact.

A regrettable case was Faxton,[3] Northants, a church with good monuments in an isolated position surrounded by fields. In 1953 the Diocese of Peterborough removed the roof and capped the walls, but by 1959 the action of the weather and of vandals had reduced it to a dangerous state so that it had to be demolished. In the same year the imposition of a Dangerous Structure Notice on the early eighteenth-century church of St Luke,[4] Old Street, London, led to the archdeacon ordering the unroofing of the building. This had to be done so quickly that the Council could not consider the matter, but the Chairman and Secretary, noting that the London DAC had agreed, concurred with this course between meetings provided that the tower and obelisk steeple were preserved. Although the building has stood roofless for nearly 40 years, the walls have recently been consolidated with joint funding from the Diocese of London and English Heritage, and there now seems to be real hope that the shell may be re-roofed and found an appropriate use.

FIG 31 *Faxton, Northants, as it was in 1946, before unroofing in 1953 and demolition in 1959. (Photograph by National Monuments Record.)*

In 1958 the Archbishops appointed a commission under the chairmanship of Lord Bridges to investigate the subject. The Council was not represented on the Commission but, in addition to giving evidence, it submitted the findings of a statistical survey of ruined and neglected churches compiled in 1954–5. The report, published in October 1960, estimated that about 370 churches were effectively redundant at that moment and that a further 420 seemed likely to become so in the next decade. Of the total of 790, 440 were buildings of considerable architectural merit or historic interest. The report's conclusions were warmly welcomed by the CCCC. 'Under the present law', the Commission found, 'one basic weakness is that there are too many procedures under which redundant churches may be demolished ... the faculty procedure is unsatisfactory for various reasons'.[5] Moreover, the statutory procedures [the Reorganisation Areas Measure and the Union of Benefices Measure] were unsatisfactory because diocesan committees did not necessarily take advice on the historic or architectural merits of the churches under review, the Church Commissioners' consultations did not always result in consistent advice, there was no provision for more than local publicity, and alternative uses were insufficiently explored.

The report therefore proposed a new Measure which would oblige Diocesan Pastoral Committees rather than the Church Commissioners to seek from the CCCC views and information about the churches under consideration, and would institute a 'waiting period' of up to three years after the declaration of redundancy during which alternative uses would be sought, after which a second scheme would provide for a suitable use, for demolition or preservation. The Measure was to establish three new national bodies – an Advisory Board for Redundant Churches to advise the Commissioners on the architectural aspects of proposals; a Redundant Churches Uses Committee (eventually established at diocesan, not national, level) to seek new uses for churches during the waiting period and a Redundant Churches Fund, financed by both Church and State, to take into care buildings considered worthy of preservation as monuments. These provisions were embodied in the Pastoral Measure 1968, now superseded by the Pastoral Measure 1983 under which the Council is obliged to prepare a 'report about the architectural quality and historic interest' of the church under review, its contents and curtilage, in the context of the other churches in the area, for consideration by the Diocesan Pastoral Committee. When the Advisory Board was appointed, Basil Clarke was amongst the first members and formed a useful link with the Council. Its present Chairman, Michael Gillingham, was for many years a member of the Council's Organs Advisory Committee, and its Secretary, Dr Jeffrey West, was formerly a member of CCC staff. The Redundant Churches Fund, of which Ivor Bulmer-Thomas became the first, extremely active, Chairman, has had several members in common with the Council such as Henry Stapleton, Dean of Carlisle, Alan Rome and Claude Blair. Confusingly renamed the Churches Conservation Trust in 1994, it now has just over 300 churches in its care.

The establishment of the Stained Glass Museum at Ely in 1970, which owed much to Margot Eates, the first Secretary of the Advisory Board, enabled threatened glass in redundant churches to be rescued either for display in the museum or for re-use elsewhere. The latter aspect of its work has since been transferred to the London Stained Glass Repository, founded at Glaziers Hall in 1984. The Council has always been represented amongst the trustees of the first organisation and on the management committee of the second. The Council also keeps in touch with the Redundant Bells Committee of the Central Council of Church Bell Ringers, the British Institute of Organ Studies and with other organisations which help to relocate objects of historic and artistic interest from redundant churches.

Between the coming into effect of the Pastoral Measure 1968 on 1 April 1969 and the end of 1994 the future of 1,422 redundant churches, rather less than one-tenth of the total belonging to the Church of England, has been settled. Of these buildings, 303 have been vested in the Churches Conservation Trust for preservation, 324 (78 of them listed) have been demolished and 795 have been found alternative uses. The CCC has in fact provided reports on nearly 1,800 churches, about 1,500 of them compiled by Donald Findlay, but in a number of cases redundancy has not been pursued. The backlog of churches noted by the Bridges Commission produced over a hundred cases each year in the early 1970s, but now a pattern of about 40 to 45 cases a year has become typical. In addition to reports on individual churches the Council has provided comparative assessments of groups of churches in Camden (Greater London), Leicester, Nottingham, Great Yarmouth and other towns and cities.

CATHEDRALS

For some time after its formation in 1949, the Cathedrals Advisory Committee occupied an anomalous position. Although a committee of the

Council, its members were appointed not by the Council, but by the Conference of Deans and Provosts in order to encourage them to refer cases to it. Many of them did. For example, the 1959 CCCC Report noted that the Cathedrals Advisory Committee had advised on the treatment of wallpaintings at Winchester and Westminster Abbey, on stonework treatment at Exeter and on possible damage by traffic vibration at Ripon and Lincoln. The first conference for cathedral architects held in 1957 'viewed with dismay the decline in numbers of architects, builders and craftsmen skilled in the special problems of repairing churches and other old buildings', which underlined the initiative taken by the CCCC following the passing of the Inspection of Churches Measure to ensure the specialist training of architects. When Will Croome, who had been Chairman since the CAC's foundation in 1949, died in 1967, he was followed by Sir Peter Scarlett, formerly Ambassador to the Holy See, then by the Duke of Grafton, who has been Chairman of many heritage organisations including the SPAB, the HCPT and the Churches and Cathedrals Committee of English Heritage, and by Michael McCrum, the present Chairman, formerly Headmaster of Eton and Master of Corpus Christi College, Cambridge. In 1973 the CAC received its first formal constitution and, although some deans and provosts were still unwilling to surrender their autonomy, they agreed at a conference in Sheffield in May 1974 that consultation with the CAC should become mandatory.

In 1967 the choice of site for a third airport for London seemed to be falling on Stansted, Essex, and the Council expressed anxiety about the effect of its expansion on neighbouring churches. Three years later, when there was anxiety that the sonic boom created as Concorde passed through the sound barrier might have damaging effects on churches under the flight path, the Cathedrals Advisory Committee persuaded the Ministry of Technology to instal monitors on cathedrals lying on the test route up the west coast of Great Britain, at Truro, St David's and Oban, particularly to calibrate the effect on stained glass and plaster. However, the findings were inconclusive. In 1985 the Council and the CAC submitted joint evidence to a parliamentary working party on the subject of damage done to historic buildings by acid rain.

One of the most important initiatives of the 1970s, which has had far-reaching effects on the conservation of historic buildings, was the establishment of the Wells Cathedral West Front Committee, under the joint aegis of the CAC and the Dean and Chapter and with Peter Burman as chairman, to find ways of rescuing the decayed thirteenth-century sculptures. Under Martin Caroe as consultant architect and Professor Robert Baker as consultant conservator, and with the advice of the Building Research Establishment, a team of trained assistants using traditional methods consolidated portions of the sculptures at risk and applied a shelter coat. Cautious experiments were also made with the use of deeply penetrating silanes. The contribution of the contemporary artist was also involved, in the replacement of the partly surviving figure of Christ in Majesty in the centre gable with a new figure carved by David Wynne.

The CAC was reconstituted in 1980 as the Cathedrals Advisory Commission for England, and under the Care of Cathedrals Measure 1991 it became the Cathedrals Fabric Commission for England. This measure also established a Fabric Advisory Committee for each cathedral, and added to the central Commission's duties a quasi-judicial role in the determination of cases. Dr Richard Gem, formerly Cathedrals Officer, became its Secretary.

NEW CHURCHES

In order to inform Church members about developments in the design of new churches, the Council organised an exhibition at the Building Centre timed to coincide with the session of the Church Assembly held in February 1956. It was opened by the President of the Royal Academy in the presence of the Archbishop of Canterbury. Later it travelled to at least 15 locations

Fig 32 *The opening of the new churches exhibition at the Building Centre, February 1956. From left: Sir Albert Richardson KCVO (President of the Royal Academy), Sir Giles Scott, OM, PPRIBA, the Most Revd Geoffrey Fisher, Archbishop of Canterbury, Frank Yerbury (Director of the Building Centre), and the Very Revd S.J.A. Evans, Dean of Gloucester (Chairman of CCCC). Photograph in CCC collection.*

in England and Wales, and then formed the basis of a collection of plans, photographs and drawings of new churches which the Council used to advise inquirers. In 1959 a pamphlet entitled *New Church Buildings: Notes on Procedure* was published by the Church Commissioners. The Council thought that it was satisfactory as far as it went, but doubted whether it would ensure a higher architectural quality for new churches. Realising that the Continent was more advanced in this field, the Council invited the distinguished German architect Herr Hermann Mäckler of Frankfurt to address that year's AGM of DAC Chairmen and Secretaries. The subject was also taken up by the newly established New Churches Research Group at Birmingham, which was particularly interested in relating the design of churches to the demands of the liturgy, at conferences in 1959 and 1960.

In the latter year it was estimated that over 180 new parish churches, as distinct from churches rebuilt after war damage, and over 220 substantial dual-purpose buildings had been erected since the war. The Council, while feeling keenly that the quality of these buildings was not always worthy of the effort made to provide them, often because of an inadequate brief, was in a difficult position as neither it nor the DACs were statutorily consulted about the design of new churches. In the case of parish churches, the Church Commissioners were required to pronounce that the structure was sound, and the archdeacon that the furnishings and ornaments were legal; there was no aesthetic scrutiny of the plans. Nor was there any check on mission churches or dual-purpose buildings. The Church Assembly therefore asked the Council to consider the design and planning of new churches, and a sub-committee was established with the purpose of preparing an outline brief and collecting a lending library of slides of churches in Britain and abroad. The Church Commissioners, estimating in 1961 that some 1,425 new buildings were still required, undertook to ensure that all plans for new churches were shown to DACs. The conclusions were presented in a handbook, *Building New Churches*.

In 1962 the New Churches Research Group became the Institute for the Study of Worship and Religious Architecture within the Faculty of Arts and Birmingham University under the direction of the Revd Dr Gilbert Cope. The absence of an English periodical to match *L'Art d'Eglise* (Belgium), *L'Art Sacré* (France), *Das Münster* (Germany) or *Liturgical Arts* (America) was to some extent met by *Maintenance and Equipment News for Churches*, published quarterly by John Catt and sent free to clergy and architects. Since 1983 it has been joined by *Church Building*, a well-illustrated bi-monthly magazine, published by *The Universe* with an editorial board composed of Roman Catholics and Anglicans, amongst whom the CCC is represented, which gives wide publicity to new churches, re-orderings and alterations to existing buildings.

In 1984 the Design and Planning Committee prepared a report *Living Stones*, on the adaptation of churches to multiple use, for debate in Synod, and a decade later, in 1994, the Council submitted to Synod a report *Mission in Mortar* showing how buildings can play an active part in the service of the Church in the Decade of Evangelism.

8
Conclusion

As this book goes to press, a newly appointed Council for the Care of Churches, the sixth since the establishment of General Synod in 1970, embarks on its term of office. Discussions are also proceeding with some urgency following the report of the Archbishops' Commission, chaired by the Bishop of Durham, on the central organisation of the Church of England, and it is certain that by the end of the quinquennium things will be very different.

The Council's report *Mission in Mortar*, presented to Synod in July 1993, argued that church buildings can and should play a vital part in the spreading of the Gospel. There will continue to be a need for responsible organisations at parochial, diocesan and national level working together to ensure that, in the words of the Archbishop of York, they prove to be keystones rather than millstones.

So having explored the past in these pages, and found with what vigour and tenacity our predecessors pursued the goal of protecting our English churches, the Council can, without vanity, claim some modest success in achieving a system of care which, given the will, has the capacity to work efficiently and harmoniously.

Nevertheless, all is still not quite as the Council would wish it to be. The Council's commitment to church archaeology is not being fully implemented; we have yet to see regular lectures on the use and care of churches included in the timetables of ordination courses, and there is still no statutory provision for either the Council or the DAC to inspect plans for new churches.

In common with other historic buildings which make up our heritage from the past, churches are more visited than ever before, and visitors, Pevsner in pocket, are better informed about architecture and art history, even if less widely schooled in what might go on within church buildings. Too many churches remain locked outside service times, for all sorts of understandable reasons. If the Council achieves nothing else during this quinquennium, it will have achieved much if the doors of England's churches can be opened wide at the millennium to celebrate the Good News of the Kingdom.

Appendix 1: Acts, Reports and Measures

Acts of Parliament
Ancient Monuments Protection Acts 1882, 1900.
Ancient Monuments Consolidation and Amendment Act 1913.
Ancient Monuments Act 1931.
Town and Country Planning Acts 1932, 1944, 1947, 1961, 1968, 1971, 1990.
Historic Buildings and Ancient Monuments Act 1953.
Local Authority (Historic Buildings) Act 1962.
Civic Amenities Act 1967.
Ancient Monuments and Archaeological Areas Act 1979.
Planning (Listed Buildings and Conservation Areas) Act 1990.
Ecclesiastical Exemption (Listed Buildings and Conservation Areas) Order 1994.

CHURCH ASSEMBLY REPORTS AND MEASURES
Report of the Ancient Monuments (Churches) Committee, 1914.
Union of Benefices Measure 1924.
First, Second and Third Reports of the Commission on the Law Relating to Faculties, 1936–8.
Faculty Jurisdiction Measure 1938.
Diocesan Reorganisation Committees Measure 1941.
New Parishes Measure 1943.
Reorganisation Areas Measure 1944.
Pastoral Reorganisation Measure 1949.
Report of the Committee on Disused Churches [1949].
Union of Benefices (Disused Churches) Measure 1952.
The Preservation of our Churches 1952.
Inspection of Churches Measure 1955.
Report of the Archbishops' Commission on Redundant Churches 1958–60, 1960.
Ecclesiastical Jurisdiction Measure 1963.
Faculty Jurisdiction Measure 1964.
Pastoral Measure 1968.

GENERAL SYNOD REPORTS AND MEASURES
Pastoral Measure 1983.
The Continuing Care of Churches and Cathedrals, 1984.
Care of Cathedrals Measure 1990.
Care of Churches and Ecclesiastical Jurisdiction Measure 1991.
Care of Churches and Ecclesiastical Jurisdiction Measure 1991: Code of Practice, 1993.

Appendix 2: Council for the Care of Churches publications

All published for the CCC by the Church Information Board of Church Assembly and its successors, unless otherwise stated; from 1972 to 1981 the CCC was known as the Council for Places of Worship. Those marked * are still in print.

1930   [Eeles], *From St Audries to Exford: The Story of an Ancient Screen and its Recovery*

1930   *Care of Churchyards*, 1932, 1936, 1952

[c. 1930] *Bells and Bellframes*, n.d.

[c.1935] Griffin, *The Care of Monumental Brasses and Ledger Slabs*, n.d., revised D'Elboux 1947, 1962

[c.1935] *Report of the Committee on the Sale of Church Plate*, n.d.

1937   *General Information on the Care of Churches*, extracted from 7th and 10th Reports, 1947, no publisher, n.d.

1939   *Churchyards and Monuments*

1940   *How to Protect a Church in Wartime: The Care of Churches and Church Goods under War Conditions*, third edition, London, Mowbray

1940   *The Lighting of Churches By Electricity*, reprinted from 8th Report, no publisher, n.d.; revised edition 1950

1945   *Loudspeakers and Acoustic Problems*, reprinted from 9th Report, no publisher, n.d. [c. 1947]

c.1945   *A Survey of Reorganisation Procedure for Diocesan Advisory Committees for the Care of Churches*, n.d.

1946   Eeles, *Wall Surfaces: Ancient Usages and Modern Care*, reprinted 1958

1947   *Lighting and Heating: Interim Notes*

1947   *The Disposal of Cremated Remains and the Construction of Columbaria*

[c. 1950] *Limewash for Church Interiors*, n.d.

1951   *The Treatment and Preservation of Monuments in Churches*, reprinted from 11th Report, London, Mowbray

1952   *Church Roof Coverings*, London, *The Builder*

1953   *Closed Churchyards*

1954   *Church Heating*

1954   *The Rural Dean's Visitation*

1955   *The Inspection and Care of Churches*

1955   *Conditions for the Installation of Electricity in Churches*, reprinted with a
        poem by John Betjeman and drawings by John Piper, 1955
1955   *The Heating of Churches*, London, The Builder House
1956   *The Moving and Re-Erection of Churches*
1956-7 *Post-War Church Buildings* [exhibition catalogue]
1957   *Organs in Parish Churches*
1957   *Parish Log Book*, London, SPCK
[c.1957] *Church Timberwork, Roofs and Fabrics: Damage and Repair*, London,
        The Builder, n.d.
1959   *The Conservation of English Wallpaintings*
1959   Milner-White, *How to Choose Stained Glass: Advice on Planning and
        Commissioning a Design*
[c.1959] *Choosing a Gravestone*, n.d.
1959   *Organ Cases for Parish Churches*
1959   *The Parochial Libraries of the Church of England: Report of a Committee
        established ... to investigate the number and condition of parochial libraries
        belonging to the Church of England*, Faith Press
1960   **How To Look After Your Church*, 1980, 1991
1960   *Faculties and the Diocesan Advisory System*, 3rd edition
[c.1960] [George], *Redecorating Churches*, n.d.
1961   *The Lighting and Wiring of Churches*, 1970, 1981
1962   [Petersen], *Altar Frontals: Their History and Construction, with special
        reference to English Tradition and Practice*
1962   *Building New Churches: Guidance for Diocesan and Parochial Building
        Committees in Briefing Architects*
1962   **The Churchyards Handbook*, revised Burman & Stapleton 1976, 1988
1962   *How To Springclean Your Church: Brief Notes for the Guidance of
        Working Parties*
1962   *Organs and Organ Cases for Parish Churches*
1963   *New Churches* [exhibition catalogue]
1964   **It Won't Happen to Us* [church insurance], 1970, 1981
1964   Edwards, *Liturgical Re-Ordering*, reprinted from 18th Annual Review
1964   Bourne, *Ecclesiologists Ancient and Modern*, reprinted from 18th
        Annual Review
1964   Evetts, *Royal Arms in Churches*, reprinted from 18th Annual Review
1965   *The Disposal of Cremated Remains*
1965   Martin, *Maintenance and Repair of Stone Buildings*
1966   Goddard, *Heating Your Church: Guidance on Choosing a New
        Installation or Modernising an Existing One*
1966   *Notes on Redecorating Churches*
1966   *Questions and Answers about Wallpaintings*, 1970

1968   An Exhibition of English Mediaeval Wallpaintings [exhibition catalogue]
1969   New Churches [exhibition catalogue]
1970   Parbrook, Sound Amplification in Your Church
1970   Economical Churchyard Maintenance
1970   Church Organs, 1985
1970   Church Inspection and Repair
1972   Barker, Wildlife Conservation in the Care of Churches and Churchyards
1973   Monumental Brasses and Brass Rubbing, with the Monumental Brass
        Society
1976   Electronic – or Pipe – Organ?, with the Royal College of Organists, the
        Incorporated Association of Organists, and the Royal School of
        Church Music
1979   Organs Advisory Committee Policy Statement
1979   The Care and Protection of Stained Glass and Other Windows in Churches
1980   *A Guide to Church Inspection and Repair, with Ecclesiastical
        Architects' and Surveyors' Association, 1995
1981   Conference on New Materials in the Conservation of Churches
1981   Code of Practice for the Conservation and Repair of Bells and Bellframes,
        with the Central Council of Church Bell Ringers
1981   Electronic Organs: Advice for Parishes, with the Royal College of
        Organists, the Incorporated Association of Organists, the Royal
        School of Church Music and the Organ Advisory Group of the
        Society of St Gregory
1982   *Recommended Practice for Repair and Maintenance of Turret Clocks in
        Churches
1982   Church Organs: Code of Recommended Practice, with the Federation of
        Master Organ Builders
1983   *Zarek, Sound Amplification in Churches, 1990
1984   *Bordass, Heating Your Church, 1996 (forthcoming)
1984   Caroe and Caroe, Stonework: Maintenance and Surface Repair
1984   *Guidelines for the Care of Textiles
1984   Turret Clocks: Automatic Winders and Drives
1985   *Loose stones: Architectural and Sculptural Fragments in Churches, with
        the Council for British Archaeology
1986   *Bristow, Redecorating Your Church
1986   *Dymond, Writing a Church Guide
1986   *Burman (ed.), Conservation of Wallpaintings: The International Scene,
        with the Cathedrals Advisory Commission for England and the
        International Centre for the Study of the Preservation and
        Restoration of Cultural Property
1987   *Mitchell-Jones, Bats in Churches

1988	*Allen, *The Protection of Churches Against Lightning*
1988	*Darby, *Church Roofing*
1989	*The Care of Church Plate*
1989	*Jeffery, *The Churchwarden's Year: A Calendar of Church Maintenance*
1989	*Brun, *Church Security: A Simple Guide*
1990	*Repair or Replace: A Guide for Parishes Considering the Future of their Organ*, with the Royal College of Organists, the Incorporated Association of Organists, the Royal School of Church Music and the Organ Advisory Group of the Society of St Gregory
1991	*Emmerson, *Church Plate*
1991	*Kerr, *The Repair and Maintenance of Glass in Churches*
1992	*Fowler, *Church Floors and Floor Coverings*
1992	*Jeffery, *Handle with Prayer: A Church Cleaner's Notebook*
1993	*The Conservation and Repair of Bells and Bellframes: Code of Practice*
1993	Mission in Mortar: The Role of the Church Building in the Decade of Evangelism: Report to General Synod
1993	*Responsible Care for Churchyards*, with the Church Commissioners
1995	*Cooper, *Wildlife in Church and Churchyard: Plants, Animals and Their Management*
1996	*Crago and Jeffery, *Safe and Sound: A Guide to Church Security*
1996	*Church Extensions and Adaptations*
1996	*Lighting Your Church* (forthcoming)
1996	*Wiring Your Church* (forthcoming)
1996	*Turret Clocks: Guidelines for Their Maintenance and Repair and for the Installation of Automatic Winders* (forthcoming)

Proformas and ring binders for *The Church Log Book* and *The Church Property Register (Terrier & Inventory)*

Looking After Your Church, video, 1991

Annual reports to Church Assembly 1927–70, and to General Synod 1971 to present

Annual Reviews (not actually issued annually) 1923–64

Newsletters 1964-78

Churchscape (annual review) 1981 to present

Appendix 3: Chairmen and Secretaries of the Council

Chairmen of the Council

1923–5	Herbert Edward Ryle, Dean of Westminster
1925–38	William Foxley Norris, Dean of Westminster
1938–53	David Herbert Somerset Cranage, Dean of Norwich
1953–72	Seiriol John Arthur Evans, Dean of Gloucester
1972–5	Michael Staffurth Stancliffe, Dean of Winchester
1975–81	Richard Shuttleworth Wingfield-Digby, Dean of Peterborough
1981–8	Thomas Eric Evans, Archdeacon of Cheltenham
1988–94	Christopher Russell Campling, Dean of Ripon
1994 to present	Colin John Fraser Scott, Bishop of Hulme

Secretaries of the Council

1921–54	Francis Carolus Eeles
1955–6	Francis Ian Gregory Rawlins
1957–71	Judith Dorothea Guillum Scott
1971–7	Desmond Christopher Mandeville
1977–90	Peter Ashley Thomas Insull Burman
1990 to present	Thomas Hugh Cocke

Notes

Most of the factual information in this booklet comes from the CCC minutes and files and, to avoid an enormous number of notes, these are not referenced.

Preface
1. James, 1984.

CHAPTER 1
1. Much of the information in these three paragraphs is adapted from Miele, 1995.
2. *Ecclesiologist*, 1.70, quoted in White, 1962.
3. For the attitude of an earlier generation, see Crook, 1995.
4. Quoted in Clarke, 1966.
5. Micklethwaite's report to the parish, quoted in *Wakefield and West Riding Herald*, 25 April 1885
6. See Addy, 'Faculty Jurisdiction in the Diocese of Chester 1660-1760' in *Churchscape*, 1982.
7. Nickalls v. Briscoe [1892], p. 269.
8. Committee for the Protection of English Churches and Their Treasures, *The Protection of Our English Churches*, first report, 1923.
9. Hansard, House of Lords, fifth series, Vol. XIV, col. 792.
10. Ibid.
11. Ancient Monuments (Churches) Committee report.
12. Ibid.
13. Ibid.
14. Ibid.
15. Ibid.
16. Ibid.
17. Ibid.
18. Eeles, 1916.
19. Typescript notes by FCE in CCC archives.
20. SPAB Annual Report for 1922.
21. This section is based on Scott, 1956, updated by revised typescript dated 1987 in CCC file.
22. Rawnsley, 1923.

CHAPTER 2
1. Anson, 1960.

2. Book of Common Prayer, 1662.
3. Information on the societies drawn from Symondson, 1995.
4. Dearmer, 1903.
5. Letter from W.A. Forsyth to FCE 29 August 1924.
6. Quoted in Dearmer, 1941.
7. Quoted in Taylor, 1992.
8. Symondson, 1991.
9. Letter dated March 1924 kindly shown to me by Father Anthony Symondson SJ.
10. Some quoted in Symondson, 1991.
11. For example in Comper, 1933.
12. Note in bound copies of *English Churchman's Kalendar* in CCC archives.
13. See Symondson, 1995
14. Note in bound copies of *English Churchman's Kalendar* in CCC archives.
15. Letter dated 5 January 1935 in CCC file on J.N. Comper.
16. Letter dated 8 January 1935 in CCC file on J.N. Comper.
17. Ibid.
18. Taylor, 1992.
19. Letter from M.N.H.C. Atchley, 8 September 1933, in CCC file on Atchley.
20. Letter from FCE to Atchley, 13 September 1933.
21. In CCC file on J.C. Bewsey.
22. Letter in CCC file on J.B.S. Comper.
23. Copy in CCC file on J.N. Comper.
24. Letter from J.B.S. Comper to FCE 9 January 1950.
25. Conversation with Miss Scott in January 1996, and Scott 1956.
26. Ibid.
27. Information from *Dictionary of National Biography*.
28. Cocke, 1995.
29. Information from obituary notice in *The Times* 29 September 1937, in Westminster Abbey Muniments.
30. Carpenter, 1966.
31. Cranage, 1952.
32. Bishop Pollock's address at the funeral service, quoted in *Norwich Diocesan Gazette*, n.d.
33. Ibid.

CHAPTER 3

1. *The Protection of Our English Churches*, 1923.
2. Ibid, 1928.
3. Ibid, 1934.

4. Eeles, 1944.
5. *The Protection of Our English Churches*, 1932.
6. *Sculptured Memorials and Headstones designed and carved in Sculptors' Studios in British Stone.*
7. Pilgrim Trust Annual Report 1934.
8. Pilgrim Trust Annual Report 1951
9. *The Preservation of Our Churches*, 1952.
10. Ibid.
11. Ibid.
12. Historic Churches Preservation Trust publicity leaflet, *c.*1954.
13. Dale, 1989.
14. CCC file: Broadhembury, St Andrew, Devon (Exeter).
15. CCC file: Porlock, St Dubricius, Somerset (Bath and Wells)
16. Letter from FCE to Hancock, 26 January 1909.
17. *English Churchman's Kalendar*, 1909.
18. *English Churchman's Kalendar*, 1932.
19. Report by A.R. Powys and P. Sturdy to the Chancellor of Bath and Wells, 13 March 1934.
20. Ibid.
21. Blacking to Caröe, 7 November 1934.
22. CCC file: Exford, St Mary Magdalene, Somerset (Bath and Wells).
23. CCC file: Attleborough, the Assumption of the Blessed Virgin Mary, Norfolk (Norwich).
24. CCC file: Bridgwater, St Mary, Somerset (Bath and Wells).
25. Comper, 1933.
26. CCC file: Ufford, Assumption of the Blessed Virgin Mary, Suffolk (St Edmundsbury and Ipswich).
27. CCC file: Gipping Chapel, Suffolk (St Edmundsbury and Ipswich).
28. CCC file: Middleton, All Saints, Essex (Chelmsford).
29. CCC file: Streatley, St Margaret, Bedfordshire (St Albans).
30. CCC file: Sundon, dedication unknown, Bedfordshire (St Albans).
31. CCC file: Winterborne Tomson, St Andrew, Dorset (Salisbury).
32. CCC file: Chingford, SS Peter and Paul (or All Saints), Greater London (Chelmsford).
33. CCC file: Stoke Mandeville, St Mary (old church), Buckinghamshire (Oxford).
34. Church Assembly, *Report of the Committee on Disused Churches*, [1949].
35. CCC file: Kennington Park, St Agnes, Greater London (Southwark).
36. See Anon, 1991.
37. Hammond, 1960.

CHAPTER 4

1. Addleshaw and Etchells, 1948.
2. Hammond, 1960.
3. See Findlay, 1985.
4. Address given at memorial service by the Revd Donald Harris, 16 May 1969 (typescript in CCC file on Rawlins).
5. See Holtby, 1991.
6. See Petingale, 1964.
7. See Lycett Green, 1994 and 1995.
8. Lycett Green, 1994.
9. Ibid.
10. Ibid.
11. Lycett Green, 1995.

CHAPTER 5

1. Binney and Burman, 1977a.
2. CCC file: Selby Abbey, Yorkshire (York).

CHAPTER 6

1. Obituary notices by Pamela Wedgwood in *The Independent*, 23 August 1990 and 19 February 1992.
2. Re St Gregory's Tredington, Fam 236.
3. Re St Mary le Bow, 1 WLR, 1363, 1365–8; the principle was derived from the observations of the Dean of the Arches in the case of St Martin in the Fields, 1970, unreported.

CHAPTER 7

1. CCC file: Salford, Christ Church, Greater Manchester (Manchester).
2. CCC file: Holnest, the Assumption of the Blessed Virgin Mary, Dorset (Salisbury).
3. CCC file: Faxton, St Dewy, Northamptonshire (Peterborough).
4. CCC file: St Luke, Old Street, Greater London (London).
5. Report of the Archbishops' Commission on Redundant Churches, 1960.

Select bibliography

* indicates that the text is an Incorporated Church Building Society booklet (mostly undated, published between the 1930s and the 1960s).
† indicates that the text is a Society for the Protection of Ancient Buildings booklet (in print c.1940).

Annual Reports
Many organisations publish annual reports which were consulted when writing this book, including the Church Commissioners, Advisory Board for Redundant Churches, Churches Conservation Trust (formerly Redundant Churches Fund), Friends of Friendless Churches, National Heritage Memorial Fund, Historic Buildings Council, English Heritage, Ancient Monuments Society, Society for the Protection of Ancient Buildings, Georgian Group, Victorian Society, Council for British Archaeology, Royal Commission on Historial Monuments of England, Cathedrals Fabric Commission for England, British Institute of Organ Studies, British Society of Master Glass Painters, etc.

Addleshaw, G.W.O. and Etchells, F., *The Architectural Setting of Anglican Worship: An Inquiry into the Arrangements for Public Worship in the Church of England from the Reformation to the Present Day*, Faber & Faber, London, 1948.
Anon, 'Diocesan Committees: Deputation to the Central Advisory Council', in *Journal of the British Society of Master Glass Painters*, Vol. III, No. 3, 1930.
Anon, 'The Faculty Jurisdiction Measure and the Craftsman', in *Journal of the British Society of Master Glass Painters*, Vol. VII, No. 4, 1939.
Anon, 'The Diocesan Advisory Committee System, Faculties and Faculty Procedure', in *Journal of the British Society of Master Glass Painters*, Vol. X, No. 4, 1950-1.
Anon, *Handbook to Lambeth Palace and Arts in the Service of the Church Exhibition*, London, 1951.
Anon, *50 Years of the National Buildings Record 1941–1991*, Royal Commission on the Historical Monuments of England, 1991.
Anson, P., *Fashions in Church Furnishings 1840-1940*, Faith Press, London, 1960.
*Architectural Requirements and Suggestions.
†Bells and Bell-Hanging in Ancient Towers.
Betjeman, J., 'Antiquarian Prejudice', in *First and Last Loves*, John Murray, London, 1952.
Betjeman, J., *Collins Guide to English Parish Churches*, Collins, London, 1958.
Binney, M., and Burman, P., *Change and Decay: The Future of Our Churches*, Studio Vista, London, 1977a.
Binney, M., and Burman, P., *Chapels and Churches: Who Cares*, British Tourist Authority, 1977b.

Bulmer-Thomas, I., 'The Ecclesiastical Exemption: I Origins', in *Transactions of the Ancient Monuments Society*, New series, Vol. 20, London, 1975.

Caroe, A.D.R., *Old Churches and Modern Craftsmanship*, Oxford University Press, London, 1949.

*Caröe, W.D., *The Care and Protection of Ancient Churches*.

*[Caröe, W.D.], *A Manual of First Aid for Archidiaconal Inspections*.

Carpenter, E.F., *A House of Kings: The Official History of Westminster Abbey*, John Baker, London, 1966.

Clarke, B.F.L., *Parish Churches of London*, Batsford, London, 1966.

Clarke, B.F.L., *Church Restoration in the Nineteenth Century*, unpublished typescript in CCC Library.

Cocke, T.H., *900 Years: the Restoration of Westminster Abbey*, Harvey Miller, London, 1995.

Comper, J.N., *Practical Considerations on the Gothic or English Altar and Certain Dependent Ornaments*, Albany Press, Aberdeen, [1893].

Comper, J.N., 'The Reasonableness of the Ornaments Rubric, illustrated by a Comparison of the German and English Altars', in *Transactions of the St Paul's Ecclesiological Society*, Vol. IV, London, 1900.

Comper, J.N., 'Further Thoughts on the English Altar, or Practical Considerations on the Planning of a Modern Church (being a continuation of a paper read to the Society in 1893)', in *Transactions of the St Paul's Ecclesiological Society*, Vol. X, Part 2, 1933.

Comper, J.N., *Of the Atmosphere of a Church*, Sheldon Press, London, 1940.

Comper, J.N., *Of the Christian Altar and the Buildings Which Contain It*, SPCK, London, 1950.

†*Cracks in Old Towers*.

Cranage, D.H.S., *Not Only a Dean*, Faith Press, London, 1952.

Crook, J.M., *John Carter and the Mind of the Gothic Revival*, Vol. 17 of Occasional Papers from the Society of Antiquaries, London, 1995.

Croome, W.I., 'Obituary: Francis Carolus Eeles', in *Journal of the British Society of Master Glass Painters*, Vol. XI, No. 4, 1954-5.

Dale, *The Law of the Parish Church*, six editions, Butterworth, London, 1932–89.

Dearmer, P., *The Parson's Handbook*, Grant Richards, London, fourth edition, 1903.

Dearmer, N., *The Life of Percy Dearmer*, The Book Club, London, 1941.

Dictionary of National Biography, compact edition, Oxford University Press, Oxford, 1975.

Eeles, F.C., *War Memorials*, Warham Guild Occasional leaflet No. 12, October 1916.

Eeles, F.C., 'The Advisory Committee System in Relation to Stained Glass', in *Journal of the British Society of Master Glass Painters*, Vol. IX, No. 2, 1944.

English Heritage Monitor, English Heritage, London, 1995.

Esher, 1st Lord, *The Early History of the Amenity Movement*, typescript of lecture given on 6 June 1957, in CCC Library.

Fawcett, J. (ed.), *The Future of the Past: Attitudes to Conservation 1174–1974*, Thames & Hudson, London, 1976.

Findlay, D.I., *All Hallows London Wall: A History and Description*, privately published, London, 1985.

Freeman, J., *W.D. Caröe: His Architectural Achievement*, Manchester University Press, Manchester, 1990.

Gill, R., *The Myth of the Empty Church*, SPCK, London, 1993.

*Goodhart-Rendel, H.S., *Commonsense Church Planning*.

Hammond, P., *Liturgy and Architecture*, Barrie & Rockliff, London, 1960.

Historic Churches Preservation Trust, publicity leaflet *c*.1954.

Holtby, R.T. (ed.), *Eric Milner Milner-White, CBE, DSO, MA, DD, LittD*, Phillimore, Chichester, 1991.

James, M.R., *The Penguin Complete Ghost Stories of M R James*, Penguin Books, Harmondsworth, 1984.

Kennet, 2nd Lord, *Preservation*, Maurice Temple Smith, London, 1972.

†*Limewash as a Stone Preservative*.

Lycett Green, C. (ed.), *John Betjeman: Letters*, Vol. I (1926–51), Methuen, London, 1994.

Lycett Green, C. (ed.), *John Betjeman: Letters*, Vol. II (1951–84), Methuen, London, 1995.

MacKechnie-Jarvis, J., *A History of the Gloucester Diocesan Advisory Committee 1919–1992*, Alan Sutton Publishing, Stroud, 1992.

*McNally, R.J., *The Regular Inspection of Churches*.

*McNally, R.J., *The Preservation of Our Churches*, 1950.

Miele, C., '"Their Interest and Habit": Professionalism and the Restoration of Medieval Churches 1837–77', in Brooks and Saint (eds), *The Victorian Church: Architecture and Society*, Manchester University Press, Manchester, 1995.

*Moore, L.T., *The Repair and Care of Medieval Churches*.

Newsom, G.H., and Newsom, G.L., *Faculty Jurisdiction of the Church of England*, second edition, Sweet & Maxwell, London, 1993.

*Passmore, H., *Church Fabric Maintenance*.

Pearce, D., *Conservation Today*, Routledge, London, 1989.

[Petingale, J.L. (ed.)], *Sir Albert Richardson KCVO, PPRA, FRIBA, MA, FSA, 1880–1964*, typescript, 1964.

Pevsner, N., *The Buildings of England* [all counties], numerous volumes and revisions, Penguin, Harmondsworth, 1951 to present.

Planning Policy Guidance 15, Department of National Heritage, 1994.

Powys, A.R., *Repair of Ancient Buildings*, J.M. Dent and Sons, London, 1929.

Rawnsley, E.F., *Canon Rawnsley*, Maclehose, Jackson and Co., Glasgow, 1923.

Scott, G.G., *A Plea for the Faithful Restoration of Our Ancient Churches*, Parker, London, 1850.

Scott, J.D.G., 'Memoir of Dr F C Eeles', in Eeles, *King's College Chapel, Aberdeen: Its Fittings, Ornaments and Ceremonial in the 16th Century*, Aberdeen, 1956.

[Scott, J.D.G.], 'Who Cares? or The Red Door in London Wall', in *Maintenance and Equipment News*, June and September 1970.

Sunderland, E.S.S., *Dibdin and the English Establishment: The Public Life of Sir Lewis Dibdin, Dean of the Arches 1903–1934*, Pentland Press, Edinburgh, 1995.

Symondson, A.N., *The Life and Work of Sir Ninian Comper 1864–1960*, Royal Institute of British Architects, London, 1988.

Symondson, A.N., 'John Betjeman and the Cult of Ninian Comper', in *The Thirties Society Journal*, No. 7, 1991.

Symondson, A.N., *Theology, Worship and the Late Victorian Church*, in Brooks and Saint, (eds.) *The Victorian Church: Architecture and Society*, Manchester University Press, Manchester, 1995.

Taylor, B., 'Church Art and Church Discipline Round About 1939', in *The Church and the Arts*, Blackwell, Oxford, 1992.

†*The Care of Wallpaintings*.

The Ecclesiastical Exemption: What It Is and How It Works, Department of National Heritage, 1994.

**The Heating of Churches*.

†*The Treatment of Ancient Buildings Damaged in War Time*.

Timms, G.B., 'The Many-Sided Influence of Percy Dearmer', article in *Church Times*, 24 February 1967.

Truman, *The Care of Churches*, Philip Allan, 1935.

White, J.F., *The Cambridge Movement: the Ecclesiologists and the Gothic Revival*, Cambridge University Press, Cambridge, 1962.

Wilkinson, A.L., 'The Diocesan Advisory Committee System, Faculties and Faculty Procedure', in *Journal of the British Society of Master Glass Painters*, Vol. XIV, No. 1, 1964.

[Winmill, J.M.], *Charles Canning Winmill: An Architect's Life*, J.M. Dent, London, 1946.